EVIL

ENGLISH 3RD SEMESTER OF BPSMV

ANJLI SEHRAWAT & ANNU SEHRAWAT

THE CONSTITUTION OF INDIA

PREAMBLE

WE, THE PEOPLE OF INDIA, having solemnly

resolved to constitute INDIA into a SOVEREIGN

SOCIALIST SECULAR DEMOCRATIC REPUBLIC

and to secure to all its citizens:

JUSTICE , social , economic and political ;

LIBERTY of thoughts , expression , belief faith and worship ;

EQUALITY of status and of opportunity ;

and to promote among them all ;

FRATERNITY assuring the dignity of the individual and the unity and integrity of the
nation ;

WE DO HEREBY GIVE TO OURSELVES THIS CONSTITUTION.

Contents

Preface

I would like to express my special thanks of gratitude to my Teacher **"Monika Mam, Sandeep Sir, Mukesh Sir, Rashmi Mam & Dr. Ashok Kumar"** who gave me the golden opportunity to do this wonderful work "write a book" , which also helped me in doing a lot of Research and i came to know about so many new things. I am really thankful to them. Words are short for expressing my gratitude to them.

A special thanks to my friend **Jyoti Dawar** and **Neetu** who always motivate me.

I am also very thankful to all my relatives and friends for their inspiration and encouragement. Words are short for expressing my gratitude to them.

Finally, I am short of words in expressing my gratitude and love to my dear & loving mother *Mrs. Sushila Sehrawat and father Narender Sehrawat* who has always inspired and encouraged me in every sphere of my life.

Foreword

BPS UNIVERSITY, KHANPUR has revised the cousre content of BA Cousre. This book has been especially written for the new syllabus of Paper Code : ENG 201.

I am sure that this book would be very useful both students and teachers suggestion and critical comments for improvement of the book are welcome.

Author

annusehrawat8520@gmail.com

9817663033

Prologue

Unit 1

Unit 2

Unit 3

Unit 4

All The World's A Stage

by William Shakespeare

All the world's a stage,
And all the men and women merely players;
They have their exits and their entrances;
And one man in his time plays many parts,

His acts being seven ages. At first the infant,
Mewling and puking in the nurse's arms;
And then the whining school-boy, with his satchel
And shining morning face, creeping like snail

Unwillingly to school. And then the lover,
Sighing like furnace, with a woeful ballad
Made to his mistress' eyebrow. Then a soldier,
Full of strange oaths, and bearded like the pard,

Jealous in honour, sudden and quick in quarrel,
Seeking the bubble reputation
Even in the cannon's mouth. And then the justice,
In fair round belly with good capon lined,

With eyes severe and beard of formal cut,
Full of wise saws and modern instances;
And so he plays his part. The sixth age shifts
Into the lean and slipper'd pantaloon,

With spectacles on nose and pouch on side;
His youthful hose, well saved, a world too wide
For his shrunk shank; and his big manly voice,
Turning again toward childish treble, pipes

And whistles in his sound. Last scene of all,
That ends this strange eventful history,
Is second childishness and mere oblivion;
Sans teeth, sans eyes, sans taste, sans everything.

All the World a Stage" by William Shakespeare (Reference to the Context)

Reference:

These lines have been taken from the poem "All the World's a Stage" written by William Shakespeare.

Context:

This sonnet of Shakespeare is from his famous play "As You Like It". This poem describes various stages of human life. Life has been compared to a play or drama played by every man and woman on the stage of the world. His seven stages of life are the seven acts of a play. This shows Shakespeare's deep knowledge and transience of human life.

Explanation: 1 -

All the world's a stage,.................................Mewling and puking in the nurse's arms.
     In the first lines of 'All the world's a stage,' the speaker, Jacques, begins with the famed lines that later came to denote this entire speech. He declares that "All the world's a stage" and that the people living in it are "merely players."

This sets up what is one of the most skilled conceits in all of English literature. Every person, no matter who they are, where they were born, or what they want to do with their lives, wakes up every day with a role. They enter, they exit, just like performers.

It's important to note at this point that these lines would be read on stage in front of an audience. The extended metaphor would not be lost on anyone listening or watching. The actor is declaring to the audience that "you" are just as much of an actor as he is.

Before the listener starts to get concerned about the role they have to play, Jacques adds that a "man," (or woman) plays many different parts in their lives, as an actor does. Whoever the actor may be on stage is not only "Jacques" he's also many other characters throughout his career. It's in the fifth line of the monologue that Shakespeare brings in a slightly more complex concept, that of the "seven ages" of humankind. The first of these is the "infant".

Explanation: 2 -

And then the whining schoolboy,...............................Full of wise saws and modern instances;

As the speech progresses, Jacque continues to describe how someone ages, the roles they play, and what everyone is like, generally, at different times in their lives. One will at some point be a "whining school-boy" and a "lover / Sighing like furnace." There will be sorrows, ballads, and losses. One will become "a soldier" and take oaths of allegiance while seeking out a fight. This is one of the more difficult stages in one's life and if drafted, not one that someone could ignore.

The man's youth has given way to a full beard like a "pard," or leopard. In these lines, there is also an interesting metaphor comparing a human or animal blowing a bubble with its mouth to staring down a cannon that might fire at any moment. Finally, this metaphorical person becomes "the justice," or magistrate, someone with a steadier knowledge of what's right and wrong. They have "Wise saws," or wise sayings and "modern instances," or arguments for legal cases.

Explanation: 3 -

And so he plays his part...sans everything.

In the sixth stage of man's life, he moves into the "pantaloon" or comfortable clothes worn by old men. His youthful clothes are too loose because he's lost weight with age. He's also lost his deep voice. It reverted back to something that's closer to what he had in one of the earlier stages of his life.

The last stage of a man's life is his "second childishness and mere oblivion." This is when he loses control of everything that made him an adult. Now, he's helpless and dependent on others, as he was when he was a child. He is "sans," or without, "taste," "eyes," and "teeth." The final image is the man without "everything." His life, all its intricate memories, and details are lost.

Summary

This poem is an excerpt (a little part or piece) from Shakespeare's famous drama 'As You Like It' . Here the poet has compared the world with a stage and human beings with actors and actresses playing different roles on this stage.

It describes the various stages of life. He counts them seven. The seven stages of life are the seven acts of play.

i. **The first stage :** Of human beings is as an infant baby. In this stage one is completely helpless, and dependent upon others, particularly upon his/her mother. This stage goes in crying, weeping and vomiting on the laps of their mothers.

v. **The second stage :** Is of a school going boy/girl. This is the time of starting learning. Parents send them to school, and the boy (or the girl) goes to school most unwillingly with his/her bag with slow steps.

v. Then comes **the third stage :**By this time s/he grows to early youthhood. This is the stage of love and romance. S/he makes love, singing songs for his/her beloved.

v.   Next, **the fourth stage :**The poet has called stage as a soldier. By this time he grows a matured responsible person. He works hard for his life, family and country. S/he is willing and trying too much to maintain his (her) reputation. Although all such reputations are only very temporary. One characteristics of this age is that he gets angry very soon.

v.   **The fifth stage :** Is the age of adulthood. By this time s/he has earned a good experience from life. Now he starts leading a fair and justified life. Physically he changes most. His belly becomes bigger than normal. Eyes become more serious. Now he is able to take lots of important decisions. This is the most powerful stage of life.

v.   By **the sixth stage :** S/he becomes an old person. Physically he becomes lean and thin. S/he learns and wants to relax from the business and worries of life. S/he becomes weaker by this time.

It is in this age that s/he prepares for the next and last stage of life, that is 'second childhood'.

v.   **The seventh and the last stage :**Of a human being is the 'second childhood'. Now s/he changes from old stage to very old age. by this time all his activities come to a stop. S/he is not able to do most things by themselves. All the glories of his life almost stop here.

His memory and eyesight become weaker. He has lost his teeth, taste and almost every thing. He becomes like a child once more, helpless and dependent upon others for his/her every little need. This stage ends in the exit form the world (in other words, s/he dies.)

i) "All the world's a stage,
   And all the men and women merely players;
   a. **What does the poet consider the whole world?**
   The poet considers the whole world **a stage.**
   b. **Why does the poet compare the world to a stage?**
   The poet compares the world to a stage **because he thought all men and women behave like the actors of a drama.**
   c. **Who are the players in the drama of life?**

All the men and women are the players.

d. **What does the wod 'Players' refer?**

The word 'players' refers **to actors.**

ii. _They have their exits and their entrances:_

And one man in his time plays many parts,

a. **What do the players have?**

The players have **their exits and entrances in the world.**

b. **What do 'they' refer?**

'They' refers to men and women.

c. **What does 'parts' refer to here?**

'Parts' refers to **characters** in a drama.

iii. _His acts being seven ages. At first the infant, Mewling and puking in the nurse's arms;_

a. **How many stages are in the life time?**

There are **seven stages** in the life time.

b. **Who is known as a nurse?**

Mother is known as a nurse.

iv. _Then the whining school-boy, with his satchel_

And shining morning face, creeping like snail

a. **Does the boy go to the school willingly?**

No, the boy doesn't go to the school willingly.

b. **Who is compared to the snail?**

The school going boy is compared to the snail.

c. **What does the boy carry to school?**

The boy carries **his shoulder bag** on his back.

v. _Sighing like furnace, with a woeful ballad_

Made to his mistress' eyebrow.

a. **How does the lover sigh?**

The lover sighs **like a furnace.**

b. **What does "woeful ballad" mean?**

"Woeful ballad" means **unhappy (or) sad song.**

Short Question Answer

Question 1: How does life begin ?

Answer : Our life begins as an infant, after we take birth. With our birth starts the first stage of our life : infancy. At this stage we are an infant baby, helpless and crying most of the time. The whole infancy spends being dependent upon others for every little needs.

Question 2 : Do you think that the whole world is a stage ?

Answer : Yes, there is no doubt that the whole world is a stage. The conception is also found in many religious and philosophical books of the world. . A human being comes to this world with certain roles to be played and duties to be fulfilled. S/he plays all the roles in this world, which acts as a stage for them. That is exactly what Shakespeare tells here.

Question 3 : Are we the actors in this world ? What roles can a person play in his her life ?

Answer : Yes, if the world is a stage, we all are actors here. We fulfil our roles assigned to us. Shakespeare talks about seven roles. They are : an infant, a complaining school boy, a lover, a bearded soldier, a wise justice, an old man, the second childhood.

Question 4 : Why does the poet compare the world with a stage ?

Answer : In a theater (or in any performance) stage is a specific place for the actors. It serves as a place where actors come and play their roles.

The poet has compared the world with a stage because here all human beings play their different roles, deliver dialogues, and fulfil their duties and responsibilities.

Question 5 : What is the first stage in a human's life? In what sense can it be a troubling stage ?

Answer : The first stage of human life is the infant stage. In this stage s/he only cries and vomits in his/her mother's arms. S/he is not able to do any thing by himself/herself.

It's very troubling stage because s/he is entirely dependent upon others. So much so, s/he is not even able to express what s/he needs. Sometimes even mothers or other caretakers get irritated because of his crying or because of taking care continuously.

Question 6 : Describe the second stage of life based on the poem.

Answer : The second stage of of life is a school going boy/girl. Now s/he is in a school going age. Mothers send them to school, which most children don't like or enjoy. S/he goes to school with his school bag most unwillingly with slow steps and always weeping, crying and complaining.

Question 7 : Why is the last stage called second childhood ?

Answer: In the final stage of his life, he changes from old to oldest age. In this stage all his activities almost come to a stop. S/he becomes extremely weaker. His/her memory, eye-sight etc. becomes very weak. S/he is even unable to perform his/her daily activities by himself. As in the first stage, in this stage also s/he becomes totally dependent upon others. So, this is like a second childhood.

Question 8 : In what sense are we the players in the world stage ?

Answer : The poet compares the world to a very big stage. Here he shows how all men and women are only actors (role players) in the drama of life.

In any drama different actors have their entries and exits, and they have assigned (allocated) roles to play. Similarly, in life drama, we have entries and exits and have our allocated roles, which we have to play. Our entries start with our birth. And, fulfilling different roles, we become very old, and exit from the world (die).

Question 9 : Who said, "All the world's a stage" ?

Answer : In Act 2, Scene 7, Line 139 of William Shakespeare's pastoral comedy As You Like It, the melancholy Jaques said the monologue 'All the world's a stage'.

Question 10 : What is the central theme of 'All the world's a stage' ?

Answer : The central theme of this monologue is life and its seven stages. Shakespeare describes the phases that are observed in a man's lifespan.

Question 11 : Why does Shakespeare call the world a "stage" ?

Answer : According to Shakespeare, the "world" is like a "stage". The stage remains permanent. Only the actors and actresses change with time. They have their parts to play. When the curtain slides down, they are no more. The stage becomes empty. It makes way for a new play, maybe the next day or the day after tomorrow. We, human beings, are like artists. We play our roles as somcone's child, lover, life partner, or grandparents during our lifespan. When our time comes, the sidewalk is our only destination leading us to the leaden death.

Question 12 : What message does 'All the world's a stage' convey ?

Through this monologue, Shakespeare gives the message of life's impermanence. How quickly the play of our life ends and the strange eventful lays are concluded get featured in this speech.

Question 13 : What does "Sans teeth, sans eyes, sans taste, sans everything" mean ?

Answer : The word "sans" is a preposition that is generally used in literary works. This word adds a flavor of humor to the line where it is used.

Literally, it means "without" or "in the absence of something". In this line, the use of palilogy (repetition of "sans") puts emphasis on the nothingness in the last stage of a human's life that is "mere oblivion".

Questions 14 : What does "Sighing like furnace" mean ?

Answer : The lover's sigh is compared to the exhausts of a furnace. A man in his youths is driven by the carnal desires that fuel his heart. It kindles the burning desire for love there. When the fire is blown out by the current of a lady's rejection, the heart sighs like a furnace. The heat of passion is there but the fire of heartfelt emotions is extinguished.

Long Question Answer

Question 1. Describe the various stages of a human's life picturized in the poem. All the World's a Stage ?

Answer : The speaker compares the world to a drama or stage. All men and woman are only actors of this world stage. We enter with our birth and exit with our death. Between the entrance and exit, we play seven roles.

The first role is of infancy. It goes in crying, weeping and depending upon others for every little need. Then, the infant grows into a school going boy. His guardians send him to school, and he goes there most unwillingly.

Thirdly, he grows into a romantic youth. He is now full of energy. He falls into love. He tries to woo his beloved by singing songs for her. In the fourth stage, the boy turns a man. He has several responsibilities, both to his family and his country. He is brave, full of enthusiasm, and seeking reputation.

By the fifth stage, he is in the role of a wise justice. He is a middle aged man now. Experiences have made him wise like a judge. He has a large stomach and a clean cut beard by now.

In the sixth stage, he is an old man. He is lean and thin, with glasses on his nose. his manly voice turns into a childish treble. Seventh is the last act. It is the 'second childhood'. He becomes very old. His memory becomes weaker. Like in the first stage, he again becomes helpless, depending upon others for his every needs.

It is now the stage of exit form the drama of life.

Question 2. : Is Shakespeare's comparison of human's life with a drama stage apt ? How ?

Answer : Shakespeare has compared human life to a play or drama played by every man and woman. He has described seven stages of life, which are like the seven acts of a play.

The comparison of the world to a stage and people to actors goes before Shakespeare. We find such comparisons made in many philosophical books too.

But, even if nobody had written about it, it is by a simple observation of life around us we find the same thing happening. Everybody takes birth, grows, and with every growth, man's life changes. He works, fulfils duties and responsibilities according to age, and finally leaves the world.

This simple observation tells us Shakespeare's comparison of human life with a drama is very apt.

Literary Devices

Shakespeare makes use of several literary devices in this speech. Some are:

Simile: 'creeping like a snail"; "soldier… bearded like the pard"; etc.

Metaphor: The entire speech itself is more like symbolism; men and women are portrayed as players whereas life is portrayed as the stage. Shakespeare uses the "stage" as an extended metaphor.

Repetition: Another figure of speech used in this monologue; words like sans, age, etc. are repeated for the sake of emphasis.

Anaphora: It is used in the eighth and ninth lines, beginning with the word "And".

Synecdoche: "Made to his mistress' eyebrow"; "And then the justice"; etc.

Alliteration: "his shrunk shank"; "quick in quarrel"; etc.

Onomatopoeia: "pipes / And whistles in his sound"

Asyndeton: "Sans teeth, sans eyes, sans taste, sans everything."

The Road Not Taken

by Robert Frost

The Road Not Taken

Two roads diverged in a yellow wood,
And sorry I could not travel both
And be one traveller, long I stood
And looked down one as far as I could
To where it bent in the undergrowth;
Then took the other, as just as fair,
And having perhaps the better claim,
Because it was grassy and wanted wear;
Though as for that the passing there
Had worn them really about the same,
And both that morning equally lay
In leaves no step had trodden black.
Oh, I kept the first for another day!
Yet knowing how way leads on to way,
I doubted if I should ever come back.
I shall be telling this with a sigh
Somewhere ages and ages hence:
Two roads diverged in a wood, and I—
I took the one less travelled by,
And that has made all the difference.

"The Road Not Taken" by Robert Frost (Reference to the Context)

Reference :

These lines have been taken from the poem "The Road Not Taken" written by Robert Frost.

Context :

The poet tells how the course of his life was determined when he came upon two roads that diverged in a wood. Forced to choose, he "took the one less traveled by, And that has made all the difference.

Explanation: -

"Two roads...travel both"

The poet while travelling on foot in the woods reaches a junction where two roads diverge. Immediately, he realizes that as a traveller travelling both the roads is impossible. Here two roads are meant two ways of life. The woods are yellow, which means that it probably falls and the leaves are turning yellow.

And be one traveler,.....................................bent in the undergrowth;

As it is impossible to travel both the roads, the poet stands there trying to choose which path he's going to take. However, the poet wants to go down both paths and is thinking about it hard. He is staring down one road, trying to see where it goes. The small plants and greenery of the woods block his view.

Then took the other,.....................................and wanted wear,

The phrase could mean something like "as just as it is fair," as in proper, righteous and equal. But this doesn't quite apply to a road. "As just as fair" is an example of a simile. Then the poet decided to check the other path because he found the other road to be less travelled and grassy one. "Wanted wear" is an example of personification.

Though as for that, ...really about the same

After travelling through the road, he found that both the roads are equally travelled. First, he found the first road to be the more travelled one, but then he says that both the roads to be equally travelled. The 'as for that" refers to the path being less worn.

And both that.....................................had trodden black

Here, again, the poet found both the paths looking same. Perhaps, he goes in the flashback. It was tough for him to recognize the real road as in the morning he was the first person to walk on the road.

He couldn't decide the right path as no step had smashed the leaves on the roads to allow him to go for the right one. These lines are an example of imagery.

Oh, I kept the first.....................................should ever come back.

The poet here saves the first road for another day. He knows how "way leads" to another, and then another until you end up very far from where you started. The poet here saves the first road for another day. Then in the third, he doesn't think he will ever be able to come back and take the other path, as much as he wishes he could.

I shall be telling this with a sigh

This line is the example of the poet's failure in choosing the right path. The word 'sigh' reflects that he is disappointed with the decision.

Somewhere ages and ....less traveled by

He accepts the fact that he is a failure in taking the right decision. 'Ages and ages' is an example of alliteration. Perhaps, he chose the less travelled one.

And that has made all the difference

The poet took the path that no one else did, and that is what has made the difference in his life that made him successful. However, a "difference" could mean success or utter failure.

Summary

This article deals with the Road Not Taken summary written by <u>Robert Frost</u> and published in the year 1916. The Road Not Taken Summary is a poem that describes the dilemma of a person standing at a road with diversion. This diversion symbolizes real-life situations. Sometimes, in life too there come times when we have to take tough decisions. We could not decide what is right or wrong for us.

Driven by our hopes and ambitions, we take a decision taken by fewer people. We think that if fail to seek accomplishments we could get a chance to change and start again. However, we travel too far and have to regret at the end. Also, it is possible that we could become an extraordinary person because of that one decision. Thus, the <u>road not taken</u> summary focuses on making wise decisions in life.

The article is all about the Road Not Taken Summary by <u>Robert Frost</u>. It explains about the road not taken summary in short. This poem signifies a situation where the poet was walking down a road that had a diversion. He had to choose between the two paths. Since he was a single person, he could choose only one of the two paths. The wood was yellow which represents a world full of people who have been residing for many years.

The poet kept standing at that fork and looked at the paths very carefully. He looked as far as he could. Before moving forward on one path, he wants to understand how it was. Was it suitable for him to walk on it or not? He was able to see the path till from where it got curved. However, afterward it was covered with trees and thus was hidden. He wanted to understand the advantages and disadvantages of the paths. The same happens in life too. We have to make decisions thinking about its good and bad consequences in the future.

The poet looked at one path for a long time to decide whether it's good or not for him. Then he takes the alternative path as he feels that both paths are equally good. He feels that the path he chose was better for him. The path was grassy which depicted that it was walked over by fewer people and also, it was 'wanted wear".

It depicted that the path was unused. However, as he walks on the path for some distance, he realizes that both the paths were similarly worn out. Even in our life, every decision has its own good and bad consequences. We might think we are in a better position than the others but it is not the reality.

The poet says that the two paths looked similar that morning. Both were having leaves on them. No one stepped on that and thus they were green. He decided to move forward on one path and keep the other for another day. Although he knew that he would not be able to return back as one path would lead to another. This happens in life too. We make a decision and move forward in that direction. We think that we would get a chance to start over again if we fail. But that does not happen.

The poet says that sometime in the future, he will take a deep breath and tell that once in a lifetime he had to take a tough decision. He was standing at a diversion of two roads. Both looked to him equally well. Thus, he decides to move forward on the road which fewer people took. As a result, it has made him what he is today. That one decision shaped his future.

Similarly, in the future, when we grow up, and then we have to say that once upon a time when you were in your youth, you have to take tough decisions. The choice made by you had made you what you are today. Thus, the article of the poem the road not taken summary gives a very strong message to the people.

It tells us to be careful in making decisions in life. One should be very wise and careful while making choices as our choices shape our future. Also, once we make a decision, it is very difficult to change and start again. One bad decision could make us regret it throughout life. All this depends on the choices we make today.

Question 1.

"Two roads diverged in a yellow wood,
And sorry I could not travel both
And be one traveller, long
I stood And looked down one as far as
I could To where it bent in the undergrowth;"

(a) What does the narrator mean by "a yellow wood"?

Answer: By "yellow wood" the poet means a forest where the trees have yellowing and falling leaves.

(b) What choice did the narrator have to make?

Answer: The narrator had to choose between the two roads.

(c) What does the narrator regret?

Answer: The narrator regrets the fact that he cannot travel on both the paths. He also regrets the fact that he cannot come back to the start once he makes a choice.

Question 2.

"Two roads diverged in a yellow wood,
And sorry, I could not travel both
And be one traveller, long
I stood And looked down one as far I could;
To where it bent in the undergrowth,"

(a) What did the narrator see in the wood?

Answer: The narrator saw two paths diverging in the forest.

b) Why did the poet stand there for "long"?

Answer: The poet stood there for long because he could not make up his mind which path to take.

(c) The poet here is using "roads" as symbols of:

Answer: Choices one makes in life.

Question 3.

"Then took the other, as just as fair,
And having perhaps the better claim,
Because it was grassy and wanted wear;
Though as for that the passing there
Had worn them really about the same,"

(a) What does "other" refer to in the above lines?

Answer: In the above lines, "other" refers to the road that was grassy and less travelled upon.

(b) Which road did the narrator choose?

Answer: The narrator chose the one that was grassy and less travelled upon.

(c) Explain "grassy and wanted wear"?

Answer: The road was covered with grass as not many people had walked this road so it was more inviting.

Question 4.

'And both that morning equally lay "
In leaves no step had trodden black.
Oh, I kept the first for another day!
Yet knowing how way leads on to way,
I doubted if I should ever come back."

(a) What does "both" refer to?

Answer: In the given lines "both" refers to the two roads that forked out in different directions.

(b) Explain the line "In leaves no step had trodden back".

Answer: The given line means a path not commonly used so the dried leaves that lay on the ground and had not been trampled upon.

(c) What made the narrator doubt whether he "should ever come back"?

Answer: The fact that one road generally leads to another made the narrator doubt that he should ever come back.

Question 5.

"I shall be telling this with a sigh
Somewhere ages and ages hence:
Two roads diverged in a wood, and I
I took the one less travelled by,
And that has made all the difference"

(a) Which road did the poet leave?

Answer: The poet left the road on which most people travelled.

(b) When will the poet look back on his life?

Answer: The poet would look back on his life after a very long time – when he is an old man.

(c) Why do you think the poet says this "with a sigh"?

Answer: The poet is regretful; he could not return and take the.road he had left behind to travel on another day.

Short answer type questions

Question 1. What was the poet's dilemma?

Answer: The poet was standing before the two roads. He had to decide which one would lead him to success. It was not easy for him to decide. So he stood there and introspected. Out the two options, he had to choose the one. Of course, it was not an easy choice.

Question 2. What was the poet's opinion about both the roads?

Answer: The poet opined that both the roads were same. They were equally travelled and there was no difference between them. So he got confused. It was difficult to decide which road would be more convenient and comfortable. He wanted to choose the one that would take him to his intended destination.

Question 3. What do the roads represent?

Answer: The roads represent the problem of decision-making. Human beings suffer because of their choices and decisions. They find themselves in such situations at every step in their lives. Out of the available options, they have to choose the one that may take them to their destination. The choice decides the outcome in life.

Question 4. Did the poet take his decision haphazardly?
Answer: No, he speculated and brooded over the situation. He took this decision after a lot of contemplation. He did not take this decision haphazardly. No doubt, he was a bit confused. After all, it was not quite easy to make the right choice. But he exercised his option after much contemplation.

Question 5. Why did the poet choose that road?
Answer: The poet chose that road because it was less travelled. He wanted to do those activities which had not been done by anyone earlier. The poet didn't seem to be interested in choosing a much trodden path of life. Avoiding the popular rat-race, he opted for the option that broke fresh grounds.

Question 6. What is the message of the poem?
Answer: The message of the poem is to make people aware of their analytical skills. The poet wishes to say that choices should be made carefully and thoughtfully. One should behave responsibly because life does not offer multiple chances every now and then.

Question 7. Did the poet make the right choice?
Answer: It is not easy to say whether the poet made the right choice or not. He, himself couldn't reach to any such conclusion. It is possible that he may repent for making such a choice. He avoided the popular and off-beaten path of life. He dared to choose the path which was less frequented used by the people. This bold decision might bring all the difference in his life.

Question 8. Why did the poet take the 'other' road? Why did the 'other' road have a better claim than the first road?
Answer: The poet had to choose one of the two roads. He left the one which was a popular choice. He decided to take the 'other' road which was less frequented and travelled by the people. The 'other' road had a better claim as it was grassy. It invited the people to walk on it.

Question 9. Describe the conditions of both the roads that lay open before the poet on that morning.
Answer: In the yellow autumnal wood, two roads diverged into two directions. Both of them were covered with the fallen leaves. In the morning, both of them were still untouched. The steps of travellers have not blackened them. One was frequently used by the travellers. The other one was not a popular choice. It seemed to invite people to walk on it.

Question 10. Was the poet certain to come back on the road he had left for another day?

Answer: Life and its ways are complex and confusing. One roads leads to another. In this web, one has to make a choice. The poet left the one road and hope that he would use it on another day. But he was quite doubtful. It often happens that the road that is left once, is left forever. Rarely do we come on to that road again.

Question 11. How does the outcome of our life depends on the choice we make to reach our destinations?

Answer: Life is full of complexities. It provides us with different choices and options. The choice is never easy. Our success or failure depends on the choice that we make. Mostly people choose the most popular or frequented paths of life. But some bold and adventurous people take risks and choose the less frequented paths and ways of life.

Question 12. What type of poem is 'The Road Not Taken'?

Answer: It is a narrative poem as it tells a story of a speaker who was struggling to choose on a morning. This poem also describes the mindset of the central character in metered verse. Besides, it is told from the first-person point of view. So, it's a lyric with a set rhyming and metrical scheme.

Question 13. Why is the poem called 'The Road Not Taken'?

Answer: The poem is titled, 'The Road Not Taken' for an interesting reason. In the poem, the road which is not taken by the speaker is the one that is interestingly similar to the other road he takes. The poet mentions the first road in the title for emphasizing the dominant thought of the speaker's mind. If there is only one road, there won't be any problem. As there are two options, he struggles to make a decision and suffers through prolonged indecisiveness. Even if he takes a path (may be suitable for him), still he will be thinking of the other one. We often think in this pattern. So, the poet advises us not to be engrossed in such thoughts.

Question 14. What does "a yellow wood" symbolize in 'The Road Not Taken'?

Answer: The phrase, "a yellow wood" symbolizes the abstract idea, change. It is also a symbol for the season, Autumn. The roads diverged in the woods. So, it means that no matter what road the speaker takes, there will be a change in his life. It is up to him how he reacts to it.

Long answer type questions

Question 1. In the poem "The Road Not Taken," what do the woods symbolize?

Answer: In this poem, the poet comes to a fork in the road where it is diversified into paths, and he must decide which path to follow. Both paths run in different directions through a "yellow wood." The poet finds himself standing in the middle and in dilemma of choosing the right path. The woods in this poem symbolize the difficulty of seeing into the future. The poet must make a choice based on limited information, since much of what he might like to see is not clear. The poet will have to rely on faith and intuition as he makes his choice, as we often must do in life. 'Woods' in the poem stand for the complexities of human life. Life is like a maze. The 'forks' stand for the 'alternatives' or 'options' life provides to reach the destination. What you reap later on in life, depends on the 'options' or the 'ways' you choose during the course of life.

Question 2. According to the poem, how does the poet feel about his or her decision in the end?

Answer: The speaker of this poem is Robert Frost himself. He is thinking about a career decision he made many years ago. He had to make a choice between seeking a secure profession which would enable him to live in comfort or to devote him to poetry and live a simple life close to nature. Same like the poet, many of us don't know whether to trust our instincts and go ahead with the pursuit of our dreams. Frost chose to devote his life to his poetry. The poet does not appear to regret the choice he made, but he sounds wistful in the last as if he wishes he knew what his alternate life would have been like if he had taken the other road.

Question 3. What is the theme or the message of the poem 'The Road Not Taken'?

Answer: Robert Frost's 'The Road Not taken' deals with the complexities of life. Life and its ways never woven in a straight line. Life provides many options. The web of life consists of many paths and sub-ways. Naturally, these complexities of life confuse a person. Out of many options and alternatives, he has to make a choice. Only a judicious choice make us reach our destination. Most of people choose the least risky and off-tradden ways of life. They don't want to take any risk. Only a few persons like the poet dare to chose a different path of like. They are bold enough to face risks and challenges in life. One has to make a choice. His success or failure in life depends on his choice. The poet chose a different path. Popular fame and fortune are sacrificed in favour of art, literature and poetry. Nobody knows what he would have gained had he followed the least risky and safe path of life.

Question 4. How does one way lead on to another? Is it easier to come back to the path we have left for another day?

Answer: Every man has his own aim or the destination of life. Life provides many options and alternatives. The zig-zag way of life is always expanding. One way leads on to another. All these additions make the web of life quite complex. These pluralities of options confuse every man. He can't follow all the ways or paths simultaneously. Amid this confusion, comes the problem of the right choice. The choice of the right or the wrong option makes all the difference in one's life. One should make a judicious choice. Success or failure in life depends on the choice you make. If the choice is made, it is rather difficult to retrace our steps. Sometimes we leave one option or alternative with the hope of coming back to it on another day. It is quite possible that we may never come back to our original position again. Hence, we must make the right choice to get the desired result and success in life.

CHAPTER THREE

The Lost Mistress

By *ROBERT BROWNING*

All's over, then: does truth sound bitter
    As one at first believes?
    Hark, 'tis the sparrows' good-night twitter
    About your cottage eaves!

    And the leaf-buds on the vine are woolly,
    I noticed that, today;
    One day more bursts them open fully
    – You know the red turns grey.

    Tomorrow we meet the same then, dearest?
    May I take your hand in mine?
    Mere friends are we, – well, friends the merest
    Keep much that I resign:

    For each glance of the eye so bright and black,
    Though I keep with heart's endeavor, –
    Your voice, when you wish the snowdrops back,
    Though it stay in my soul for ever! –

    Yet I will but say what mere friends say,
    Or only a thought stronger;
    I will hold your hand but as long as all may,
    Or so very little longer!

"The Lost Mistress" by <u>ROBERT BROWNING</u>(Reference to the Context)

Reference :

These lines have been taken from the poem "The Lost Mistress" written by Robert Browning.

Context :

In "The Lost Mistress" is a Dramatic Monologue by Browning. In the poem, the poet represents the passion of grief. The speaker is a lover. But next morning his beloved is going to be somebody else's wife. She has come to meet him at night and he says that their love has come to bites and at last it is a fact, although a bitter one. The sparrows are twittering near her cottage.

Explanation -

All's over, then:..About you cottage eaves!

The speaker of these lines is a rejected lover. He has lost his mistress. He says that all between them is over. He says that the truth sounds bitter at first sight. But there is no sense of bitterness in his heart for his sweetheart. He asks his beloved to listen to the twittering of sparrows on the eaves of his cottage. The twittering of sparrows signifies good night to him and his beloved. Through the sparrow's twittering of good night, he tries to assure himself that there is still a ray of hope in his life because night is followed by morning. Now their relationship is over but they can form a new relationship in the morning. Thus all is not over for the lover.

And the leaf-buds.....................................the red turns grey.

In these lines, the lover tells his beloved that the leaf-buds on the vine are soft and smooth. He noticed during the day that the buds will turn into flowers in a day. But the flowers are very short-lived. After sometime the flowers will turn grey. It means they will wither away after sometime. Through the allusion of greying of flowers, the lover is trying to convey the message that this is the cycle of nature. Everything which takes birth will die one day. But, he further says that just as spring brings life to flowers on the vine, in the same way, their dead relation will be brought to life. Their relationship assumes a new form, the form of friendship. There is no sign of bitterness in the nature of the lover.

To-morrow we...much that I resign:

The lover's sweetheart rejected him. He accepts this fact without bitterness. He asks his beloved to allow him to meet her. He seeks her permission to hold her hand for some time. He tells his beloved that he just wants to be his friend, nothing more. Here, what lover trying to say is that if the love relationship between them is not possible then they can remain at least mere friends. These lines show the optimism of the lover.

For each glance...my soul forever!

The lover knows that all is over. Yet he is not hopeless. He is tactful. He tried many tricks to persuade her. He praises her. He says that your bright and black eyes create a permanent impression in my heart and when you desire for a snowdrop your sweet voice keep echoing in my heart. The memory of your eyes and your voice will stay forever in my soul. By praising her he just wants to win her back. He does not want to lose her.

Yes, I will but...very little longer!

The lover knows that all is over. There is nothing left between them. But he does not lose hope. In the end, he tells his beloved that he will say her only such things which a friend can say to each other. He will feel satisfied even if they can remain mere friends. He seeks her permission to hold her hand for some time just as a simple friend. But then he hopes that perhaps he will be able to hold the hand of his beloved for a little longer time. Perhaps after sometime, this friendship will turn into a relationship of love. Thus we can say that he is very hopeful.

Summary

The Lost Mistress Written by Browning is a Dramatic Monologue. It is dramatic monologue because throughout the poem a single character speaks. It is a talk by a single person. Throughout the poem, the speech of the speaker is directed to a person who remains silent. The speaker of the poem is a person who loves a lady. But the lady refuses the proposal of his love. He accepts his refusal without bitterness. He is a great optimist. He keeps hoping against hope. He has no feeling of bitterness towards his beloved. He is neither angry nor annoyed. He knows that their love relationship has come to an end yet he is hopeful. He says that he will be satisfied even if they can remain mere friends. He says that the truth sounds bitter at first sight.

He asks his beloved to listen the twittering of the sparrow on the eaves of his cottage. The twittering of the sparrows signifies good-night to him and his beloved. Through the sparrow's twittering of good night, he tries to assure himself that there is still a ray of hope in his life. The night is followed by morning. And morning is a symbol of a new beginning. They can also begin with a new relationship, the relationship of friendship. Thus all is not over. The lover tells his beloved that the leaf-buds on the vine are soft and smooth. He noticed during the day that the buds will turn into flowers in a day. But the flowers are very short-lived. After sometime the flowers will turn grey. It means they will wither away after sometime. He says that this is the cycle of nature.

Everything which takes birth will die one day. But just as spring brings life to flowers on the vine in the same way their dead relationship will be revived. Their relationship assumes a new form, the form of friendship. The lover is tactful. He tries many tricks to win her back. He asks his beloved to allow him to meet her. He seeks her permission to hold her hand for some time. He tells her that the only thing he wants, is, her friendship. What the lover here is trying to say is that if the love relationship between them is not possible then they can remain mere friends. He says that he will never forget her black and bright eyes. He will never forget her sweet voice. The memory of her sweet voice and bright eyes will always remain in his memory. Finally, he seeks her permission to hold her hand for some time just as a simple friend. Then his hope grows bigger. He hopes that perhaps he will be able to hold the hand of his beloved for a little longer time. He hopes that perhaps after sometime this friendship will turn into a new relationship- the relationship of love. The persona keeps hoping against hope. He is a great optimist.

Questions-Answer (Short Type)

Q. 1. 'All's over then'. What is over?

Ans:- All's over then' are the opening lines of Robert Browning's dramatic monologue named "The Lost Mistress". These lines are uttered by a lover. He loves a lady passionately. But she rejected his love. Now there is nothing left between them. Their love relationship has come to an end. All the doors of lady's heart are now closed. He uttered these words after being rejected. He says that all is over. There is nothing left between him and his beloved. He is totally rejected.

Q.2.: How does the speaker 'interpret: Sparrow's good-night twitter'.

Ans.:- "The Lost Mistress" is a poem about a lover who has lost his mistress. She rejected his love proposal yet he is hopeful. He has no feeling of bitterness in his heart for his beloved. He wants to win her back. He asks his beloved to hear the twittering of sparrow's on the eaves of his cottage. It appears to him that the twittering of sparrows signifies good night to him and his beloved. He calls it a good night twitter. He says that they are parted only for a night. And the night is followed by morning. Morning is a symbol of beginning. He hopes that in the morning his relationship will also take a new form. Through the good night twitter, he tries to assure himself that there is still a ray of hope in his life. He hopes of making a new relationship with his beloved.

Q. 3.: What does the lover say about the lost mistress's glances and voice?

Ans.:- The lady has rejected the love proposal of the lover but he is hopeful. He is a tactful person. He tried tricks to win her back. He started praising her. He says that he will miss many of his beloved if they part their ways. He will miss the glance of her black and bright eyes. He will also miss her sweet voice. The memory of his bright eyes and sweet voice will always remain in his soul. He will never forget her. By praising her physical charms he trie to win her love back.

Q. 4. What does the symbol of 'greying' and 'flowers' signify?

Ans.:-Through the symbol of greying of flowers, the lover is trying to convey to his beloved the cyclical nature of the universe. Everything which takes birth will die one day. It is the cycle of the universe. Poet says that the leaf – buds on the vine are soft and smooth. He <u>notices</u> during the day that after one day these buds will turn into flowers and after some time the flowers will turn grey. It means the flowers will wither away. He says that just like flowers their love relationship has come to an end. So through the symbol of flowers, the poet depicts the cycle of nature.

Q. 5. What sort of relationship does the speaker hope to establish with The Lost Mistress.

Ans. "The Lost Mistress" is the poem about a lover who has lost his mistress. Their love relationship has come to an end. Now there is nothing left between them. He accepts this rejection with hope in his heart. He is a great optimist. He keeps hoping against hope. He knows that their love relationship is over. He now wants to build a new relationship with his beloved-the relationship of friendship. He says that now there is no relationship between him and his beloved but they can at least keep a relationship of friendship. He says that he will be satisfied even if they can remain friends. So he hopes to establish the relationship of friendship between him and his beloved.

Long Type Question

Q. 1. Discuss "The Lost Mistress" as a dramatic monologue.

Ans.:- The dramatic monologue is perhaps the only poetic art form used by Browning. This form is dramatic in the sense that the narrator is not the poet but the character created by him. It is a monologue because throughout the poem a single character speaks. It is a talk by a single person. "The Lost Mistress" is also a dramatic monologue. It is dramatic because the presentation is impersonal. Browning speaks through a character. The character in the poem is an unsuccessful lover who speaks in the form of a monologue. Browning's dramatic monologues are, essentially, psychological studies of the narrators. Their basic purpose is to lay bare the soul of the narrator at every step. Browning shows a deep psychological insight in depicting the inner working of the lover's mind. This is perhaps one of the major characteristics of Browning's monologues. The lover in the poem has lost his love. His sweetheart rejected him. He himself tells that everything between them is over. Yet he is neither angry nor annoyed. His heart is not broken. He says that now there is no love between him and his beloved. But he will be satisfied even if they can remain more friends. The lover asks his beloved to hear the twittering of sparrows on the eaves of his cottage. The twittering of sparrows signifies good night to him and his beloved. The leaf- buds are soft and smooth. After one day these buds will turn into flowers and after some time the flowers will turn grey. Everything on this earth which takes birth will have to die. This is the cycle of nature. In the same way, the love between lover and his beloved has come to an end. But the lover keeps hoping against hope. He asks his beloved to allow him to meet her next day. He seeks her permission to hold her hand for sometime. He says that he will be contended if they remain merely friends. Then he says that he will never forget the glances of black and bright eyes of hers. He also praises her sweet voice. He tells her that he will never forget her. Her memory will stay forever in his soul. By praising his beloved, the lover just wants to show the depth of his love for her. In the end, he tells his sweetheart that he will say her only such things which a friend can say. He just wants to be allowed to hold her hand as a friend. At the same time, he wants that perhaps he could be able to hold her hand a litter longer. Thus the monologue, like many other monologues of Browning ends on a note of optimism.

Thus we can say that "The Lost Mistress" fulfil all the requirements of a dramatic monologue. This poem is a perfect example of a dramatic monologue genre.

Q. 2. The lover in the poem continues hoping against hope. Elaborate.

Ans:- Browning was one of the greatest philosophic poets in the whole range of English poetry during the nineteenth century. Optimism is the basic element of Browning's philosophy. He has also been called an "incorrigible" optimist. Almost all his poems show his optimistic outlook on life. "The Lost Mistress" is filled with robust optimism. The lover in this poem like the lover of "The Last Ride Together" never loses hope. It is a poem of rejected love yet of boundless optimism. In the beginning, the lover says that everything between him and his beloved is over. The love between them has come to an end. He has lost his mistress yet he is not prepared to accept the harsh reality of these hopeless situations. He is not feeling bad. His heart is not broken. He never curses his beloved. The lover continues hoping against hope. He fells his beloved that he will be satisfied even if they can remain merely friends. He seeks her permission to hold her hand for some time just as a simple friend. The only thing he wants now is a simple friendship. With his beloved then he starts praising his beloved. He says that he will never forget the black and bright eyes of his beloved. He praises her sweet voice. He says that he will never forget her sweet voice. He also tells her that he will never forget her and his memory will always remain in his soul. By praising her he just wants to show her how much he loves her. He lays bare his soul to show the intensity and depth of his love for her. He wants to build a new relationship, the relationship; of friendship. He wants to hold her hand just as a mere friend for a little time. But in the end, his hope grows bigger. He hopes that after some time he will be able to be a little more closely than a simple friend. First, he wants to hold her beloved's hand just as a mere friend but now he wants to hold her hand a little longer than held by a mere friend. The shift from mere to merest shows lover's optimism. The poem like many other love poems ends on a note of optimism. The lover despite losing his beloved does not want to lose hope. He keeps hoping against hope and this is the basic characteristic of Browning's philosophy.

Woman Work

by Maya Angelou

I've got the children to tend
The clothes to mend
The floor to mop
The food to shop
Then the chicken to fry
The baby to dry
I got company to feed
The garden to weed
I've got shirts to press
The tots to dress
The can to be cut
I gotta clean up this hut
Then see about the sick
And the cotton to pick.

Shine on me, sunshine
Rain on me, rain
Fall softly, dewdrops
And cool my brow again.

Storm, blow me from here
With your fiercest wind
Let me float across the sky
'Til I can rest again.

Fall gently, snowflakes
Cover me with white
Cold icy kisses and
Let me rest tonight.

Sun, rain, curving sky
Mountain, oceans, leaf and stone
Star shine, moon glow
You're all that I can call my own.

"Woman Work" by Maya Angelou (Reference to the Context)

Reference:

These lines have been taken from the poem "Woman Work" written by Maya Angelou.

Context:

The poetess feels extremely bored and tired after attending to her house-hold affairs. She feels that only the natural phenomena can exercise healthy influence on her. The natural objects can save her from unbearable boredom and can raise her spirits. A house-hold woman remains awfully busy with the domestic chores. Even then, she can enjoy nature through her imagination. It is an indirect praise of the woman's greatness. In general, the poem is an escape from the drudgery of the mechanical routine and taking shelter in ideal life.

Explanation -

I've got the...........................The food to shop
    In these lines, the poetess describes the life of a domestic woman, whose life is very hard because she has to do a lot of household activities. She has to care for her offspring. She has to repair their clothes. She has to buy food

for her family.

It means that she is an active member of her family because she is involved in domestic chores from morning to evening. These lines show her responsible and active nature. She uses assonance(repetition of vowels) in the starting stanza like tend, mend, and mop, shop.

The poem presents the modern mechanical age that has given everything to man but not mental satisfaction and calm. The language of the poem is very simple but has a pragmatic approach.

Then chicken to...garden to weed

In these lines, the poetess is counting some of her household duties which she has to perform daily. She has to fry chicken and cook food for the family. She has to bathe, dry, and clothe the babies. She also has to look after a number of guests whom she has to entertain.

She has to look after and take care of the back lawn or the backyard ground, otherwise, the plants there would die away. This is a reaction to the thankless tasks of the household. The poetess has expressed her thoughts about the place of women in our society.

I've got the.................................clean up this hut

These lines tell us about a domestic and common woman. Being a responsible member of the family, a domestic woman has to iron the clothes of her family. She has to change the dress of her little children many times a day.

She has to trim the little plants in her house to make them beautiful and attractive because it is her duty to keep the house clean. These lines reflect that woman who gets busy all the time ignoring her aesthetic side of life.

Shine on me,.................................cool my brow again

These lines express the domestic woman's inner side and inner feelings. She calls the elements of nature for her help because she has got tired after doing a lot of work at home. She beseeched the sun to pour its sunlight on her because its rays are a source of energy.

She calls the rain to fall on her forehead to make her cool because the water of the rain gives freshness to her body and mind. She addresses the dewdrops to fall on her softly and to cool her hot mind. The poetess describes the boring condition of a domestic lady. She laments that her domestic busy life has deprived her of the company of sunshine, rain, and dewdrops. She intends to make her warm with sunlight and cool with rain.

Storm, blow me.................................I can rest again

Here the poetess says that a domestic woman is so much fed up with the monotony of her household life that she wants to escape from such a life. She expresses her yearning to be in the company of the objects of nature.

She beseeched the storm to come to her and take her with its intense winds from there so that she may be free for a while from her monotonous routine. She requests the storm to take her from there and leave her across the skies so that she may keep floating there and be satisfied.

The elements of nature provide her perfect rest and peace of mind. The dull and drab routine of her life fails to suppress her creative impulse and disconnect her from the company of nature. She adores the elements of nature and wants to enjoy their company.

Fall gently, snowflakes...**rest to night**

The poetess has already enumerated the list of her daily assignments being a housewife. Her detail shows that she has been living like a prisoner in her house under the commands of her husband and the demands of her children.

She wants to get herself relaxed with the touch of cold icy wind. The more she is covered gently with the snowflakes, the more she will feel comforted. Her escape into snowfall will give her both shelter and rest.

Sun, rain, curving...**I can call my own**

These lines express the wishes of a domestic woman. She wishes to be in the company of natural elements. She is passionate to be among mountains, oceans, leaves, stones, star-shine, moon glow for refreshment. She longs to sit in the company of all these natural objects.

She wants to give herself relief from painful and hectic responsibilities. She does not feel happy doing domestic chores. Her life is without any charm and pleasure. Her duties in the house, are very tedious and painful

The use of the word mend, mop, and shop shows her engagement during the day. She works without rest and relaxation. Time has bowed her down to compromise with the dull and dreary life of daily work.

Summary

"Woman Work" is a very domestic poem depicting the typical routine life of a woman who performs her daily chores effectively and then yearns for a fantastic break amidst the elements of nature to give her strength and comfort.

As a housewife, she has to perform many chores. She has to tend her children, mend their clothes, mop the floor and do some shopping for their meals. Then she has to fry chicken, dry the baby, feed her animals, weed off her garden, press the shirts, dress her tots, cut the canes and clean up her whole house to make it beautiful and appealing.

This is the drudgery of her routine, which makes her life so monotonous and prosaic; but the woman in the poem is an idealist and wants to go in the lap of nature to give her relief and comfort. She calls forth the sun, the moon, the mountains, cold ice, and the curving sky to take her away into the space so that she can fly there, forget her neck-breaking routine, and feel the freshness of natural elements to stimulate her body and soul to once again perform the next day's chores.

Questions - Answers

Question 1. Trace the elements of postcolonialism in Maya Angelou's poems.

Ans. Perhaps a very universal idea when it comes to postcolonialism is that of the empire writing back. In her poem *Still I Rise,* Maya Angelou writes back. She writes back to those who have oppressed her and her voice, and she writes back against the culture of oppression.

A similar yet distinct idea is explored in *Phenomenal Woman.* She breaks out of the patriarchal bonds that tie her to a stereotypical idea of what a woman should be and explores her own femininity. In *Women Work,* Maya Angelou confronts the culture of colonialism head-on, writing about the double colonization of woman and talking about the themes of slavery and gender inequality at the same time. The element of postcolonialism comes through rather forcefully in this poem, as she challenges all the evils of colonialism in the length of a single poem.

Question 2. How can Maya Angelou be understood as a feminist poet?

Ans. One of the central themes explored by Maya Angelou is that of gender inequality. While her poems are not limited by gynocentric concerns, woman's issues are a big part of her writing. In *Phenomenal Woman,* Maya Angelou celebrates self-definition and womanhood, talking about her femininity with pride. A similar sentiment is echoed in *Still I*

Rise, in which she writes against oppression, and celebrates the spirit of resilience within women.

Even in poems like *Woman Work,* Angelou writes about woman's issues and inequality and fiercely condemns gender discrimination, delineating woman as a slave.

Question 3. How does the theme of slavery operate in *Woman Work*?

Ans. A very potent and pervasive theme in the poem *Woman Work* is the that of slavery. The poet mentions picking cotton, a clear indication of an underlying slave narrative. She talks about the fact that being a woman is like being a slave. She harshly condemns both slavery and gender inequality. She talks about how dire the conditions of the slave/woman are. With her use of vivid imagery, Maya Angelou effectively weaves a narrative that can be seen as a slave narrative.

Question 4. Why does the working woman in the poem, Woman Work make a passionate appeal to nature?

Ans: Woman Work is a beautiful poem written by Maya Angelou. In this poem, she tells the readers about a serious and important fact about those women who pass their lives in doing house-hold chores. Such a woman is being represented by the poetess herself. She calls the elements of nature to get freshness from their company. She wants to enjoy the warmth of sunshine and the coolness of rain. She wants to feel the cool and soft-touch of dew-drops on her face. **Fall gently snowflakes, And cover me with White, let me float across the sky, Till I can rest again.**

The domestic woman calls the elements of nature because the members of her family do not treat her well. She wishes to be in the company of her past friends like sun, rain, mountain, oceans, leaves, star-shine, moon glow for refreshment and peace of mind.

Mountains, oceans, leaf and stone Star shine, moon glow
You are all that I can call my own

The poetess has personified different objects of nature to show their importance. Therefore, the household woman wants to enjoy rain, sunshine, mountains, and snowflakes to overcome her monotony and boredom.

She needs a break to refresh herself. She knows that *Nature has a healing effect.* Between the lines, she is criticizing the male-dominated world. She means that these natural objects are beneficial for all creatures without discrimination.

Question 5. The poem Woman Work deals with the boredom felt in our daily life and especially of woman. Discuss.

Ans: This poem has been written by Maya Angelou. She is a living poetess. Most of her poetry deals with the problems and status of women in male dominant society. In this poem, she describes the routine life of a domestic woman.A housewife remains busy in her domestic chores. She performs her all responsibilities without any complaint. But her routine life has made her rebel. She intends to enjoy the company of nature.

She is not satisfied with her family members. She rejects the male dominant society and shows her love for natural objects. She thinks that only nature and its aspects can provide her mental and physical pleasure.

She invokes the natural objects to enjoy rain, sunshine, dewdrops, and gentle flakes of snow. A domestic woman is so much tired of the monotony of her household life that she wants to escape from such a life.

She requests the storm to take her away from her dull and colorless world. She seems to be tired of the daily routine of life. She wants to reach some remote corner of the world where she can enjoy some moments of rest, peace, and pleasure again.

She desires to take a rest for some time in the company of nature. She wishes to fly with a storm wind into the open sky. She wishes to be among mountains, oceans, leaves and stones, starshine, and moonlight. She wants to change her dull and boring life into a charming adventure.

CHAPTER FIVE

Where The Mind Is Without Fear

by Rabindranath Tagore

Where the mind is without fear and the head is held high
Where knowledge is free
Where the world has not been broken up into fragments
By narrow domestic walls
Where words come out from the depth of truth
Where tireless striving stretches its arms towards perfection
Where the clear stream of reason has not lost its way
Into the dreary desert sand of dead habit
Where the mind is led forward by thee
Into ever-widening thought and action
Into that heaven of freedom, my Father, let my country awake.

'Where the Mind is Without Fear' by Rabindranath Tagore(Reference to the Context)

Reference :

These lines have been taken from the poem **"Where the Mind is Without Fear"** written by **Rabindranath Tagore.**

Context :

These lines have been taken from the poem "Where the Mind is without Fear" by "Rabindranath "Rabindranath Tagore" Tagore". The poet prays to God that his country India should be a heaven of freedom.

Explanation:

Where the mind...towards perfection.

The poet prays to God that there should be an atmosphere of fearlessness. Knowledge should be free for all. The country men should not be divided over caste and creed. People of the country should speak the truth and be God blessed to have a perfect life. They should not get tired of working.

Where the clear...let my country awake.

The poet prays to God that Indians should be logical & progressive in thoughts & actions. They should have the power to reason out the bad and useless useless customs customs. Only God can help by guiding the people. God should make India a paradise on earth.

Central Idea

This poem is a reflection of the poet's good and ideal nature. He has utmost faith in God. He prays to God with all his heart that He should guide the countrymen to work hard, speak the truth, be forward forward and logical logical in approach. Rabindranath Tagore aspires to see the country and his people to be in peace and prosper. He loves his country a lot and wishes for its welfare.

Summary

"Where The Mind Is Without Fear" is a pre-independent poem in which the poet sincerely urges to God to awake his fellow beings for the realization that the essential need to live in a free and united country. He wants his countrymen to awake and enjoy the life of full dignity and honour.

His countrymen would not be superstitious or believers of blind faith rather than they would lead the life of enlightened and educated.

He wishes to the people, to be honest, open-minded and industrious. Then only they would stretch their **'arms towards perfection'** and the nation can actually achieve the apex of success.

They need to use their reasons over their blind faiths and must be ready to accept new thoughts and ideas. He requests God to free his country from manipulation, corruption, and slavery. He yearns for an awakened country where there would be freedom of the mind and expression of ideas.

The poem invokes the deep patriotic feelings. Our country is subjugated by castes, creed, superstitious beliefs and biased ideas. Tagore earnestly appeals to God that a country would be where people's **'head is high'** and **'knowledge is free'**.

His country would not be divided and fragmented into pieces due to their narrow thoughts. They should express their words not from the mind but from **'the depth of truth'** and heart.

He urges God to guide his countrymen for moral awakening to fight for their rights against British inhuman rules. Liberate them from the fear of oppression, repression, and subjugation. Unshackle the chains of fear and direct them to the paths of progress and prosperity.

They should be confident not confined. There would not be injustice and inequality in the country on the basis of caste, creed, and gender.

Countrymen should be unprejudiced and open-minded accepting the new challenges and changes. They should lead their lives of decency and dignity.

To conclude "Where The Mind Is Without Fear" is a poem in which Tagore reveals his personal quest for the Divine and characterized by a variety of original themes both in thought and expression.

Therefore, this poem is remarkable to a great extent which expresses the intensity of the feeling of freedom. His poem is universal in its appeal and envisions the 'heaven of freedom' and happier future for mankind.

Short Question Answer

Question 1. What is meant by 'mind is without fear'?

Ans: The expression 'Mind is without fear' insinuates the fact that our minds should be courageous. We ought not to be overwhelmed by the shackles of tyranny and oppression. Dread should not be able to discourage us. Our heads should be held high, with no type of dread or confinement.

Question 2. Explain: 'head held high'.

Ans: 'Head held high' signifies to have confidence. The heads of the countrymen are held down as a result of the horrifying mistreatment suffered by them in the hands of the British. The poet wants their heads to be held high with most extreme pride and poise and not bowed down.

Question 3. Whose mind is the poet talking about and why?

Ans: The poet is discussing the minds of the countrymen. He wants his comrades to be courageous and not remain grasped in dread. His comrades were under the grip of the British when he composed this poem. So his vision is of a daring India.

Question 4. What is the vision of the poet?

Ans: The poet envisions a' World of Freedom' that can be acquired only if the people are fearless. Only a fearless mind can keep upright and straight his head. He wrote this poem when the British controlled the Indians. So, without any internal domination, he visualizes a mental image of free India without any external hegemony.

Question 5. Why does the poet feel that his countrymen should not feel any kind of fear?

Ans: The poet knows how magnificent India used to be in the past, how India soared high before its views were chained. With the advent of the British, the people had lost their pride, confidence, and self-esteem. So the poet dreams of a free nation where his countrymen would not feel any kind of fear or oppression. People would keep bravely their heads high and voice their opinions freely.

Question 6. How would the countrymen be able to hold their heads high?

Ans: The countrymen would be able to keep their heads high if they were free from any kind of oppression. They would derive power from their access to knowledge that could assist them to become confident. Their knowledge would not be confined to small thoughts and ideas. Narrow walls would bind them into chains, all of which would assist them to keep their heads high.

Question 7. Explain 'Where knowledge is free'.

Ans: Knowledge enables us to comprehend different things, and everyone has the right to acquire knowledge regardless of caste, creed, and status. The sentence' Where knowledge is free' occurs in the poem

Where the Mind is Without Fear by Rabindranath Tagore. The poet wanted an atmosphere in which knowledge would be freely available to everyone and not limited to a specific segment of society. Not only the wealthy and wealthy parts should be provided with the chance to gain understanding. It should be accessible to everyone, whether the rich or the poor, without any social obstacles of any kind. It should not be limited by narrow ideas and social backwardness because it is only the light of knowledge that can obliterate the darkness of ignorance.

Long Question Answer

Q.1. How does Rabindranath describe the present state of his country?

Ans. The poet is very much dissatisfied with the present state of his country. He finds that an atmosphere of fear prevails throughout the country. The minds of the people are chained by ignorance. People also suffer under the dead weight of old, outdated customs. A thousand barriers of caste, creed and religion create disunity among the people. Ignorance and superstitions have paralysed our reason and judgement. There are a thousand barriers to knowledge. Thus the people are prevented from seeking knowledge and truth. And, even when they arrive at the truth of something, fear prevents them from openly expressing it. In short, the unfortunate people of our country have forgotten that they are human beings. They live the life of beasts under the dark shadow of fear and ignorance.

Q.2. Explain in your own words the kind of freedom that Rabindranath wishes his country to achieve.

Ans. In the poem **Where the Mind is without Fear**, the poet prays to God to wake his country into a world of ideal freedom. The whole poem is an exposition of what the poet means by this freedom.

The poet wishes that knowledge should be free in his country. He further wishes his countrymen to be free from the dead habits of custom. In that world of freedom, truth will reign supreme and everyone will strive towards perfection. In that country of ideal freedom, reason will not be swallowed by dead customs. In that world of freedom, the people, in their thoughts and actions, will be led by God himself. This is the kind of freedom the poet wishes his country to achieve.

Q.3. State briefly the poet's ideal of true freedom.

Or

For what kind of freedom does the poet pray to God for his motherland, India?

Ans. The poet prays to God for true freedom for his country and countrymen. This freedom does not mean mere emancipation from foreign rule. It is the moral and spiritual freedom of man. Men of a truly free country are without fear, without narrow prejudices. They are noble. dignified and disciplined. They can acquire knowledge without any hindrance and speak out the truth without any hesitation. In a truly free country men unceasingly try to achieve perfection in the varied fields of thought and action. This is the poet's idea of true freedom and he invokes the Supreme Father to awaken his motherland into this heaven of freedom.

Q.4. Describe the qualities of the mind of man in a truly free country.

Or

What does the poet say about the mind of men of a truly free country?

Ans. In a truly free country, the mind of men must be fearless and must be free from all prejudices and superstitions. In such a country, the mind seeks knowledge freely. In an ideal state of freedom the mind strictly adheres to reason without paying any heed to old customs and conventions. There the human mind is sincere, outspoken, and it untiringly tries to attain perfection in every field of life. The poet also wants great adventures of the mind into boundless realms of thought and action under the divine guidance of the Supreme Father.

CHAPTER SIX

Palanquin Bearers

by Sarojini Naidu

Lightly, O lightly we bear her along,

She sways like a flower in the wind of our song;

She skims like a bird on the foam of a stream,

She floats like a laugh from the lips of a dream.

Gaily, O gaily we glide and we sing,

We bear her along like a pearl on a string.

Softly, O softly we bear her along,

She hangs like a star in the dew of our song;

She springs like a beam on the brow of the tide,

She falls like a tear from the eyes of a bride.

Lightly, O lightly we glide and we sing,

We bear her along like a pearl on a string.

'Palanquin Bearers' by Sarojini Naidu(Reference to the Context)

Reference :

These lines have been taken from the poem "**Palanquin Bearers**" written by **Sarojini Naidu.**

Context :

The theme of the poem "palanquin bearers" by "sarojini naidu" is to reflect about the Indian marriages and their cultures. The poet has deliberatory used the contradictory feeling of laughing and weeping. The bride is sad and is crying as she is separated from her family. But simultaneuosly she is also overjoyed as she is starting a new family.

Explanation -

Lightly, O lightly we bear her along,
The pellucid style and the cadence of a collective song fill the ambiance of "Palanquin Bearers". Naidu speaks in this poem from the perspective of the bearers carrying a lady to a place. She does not delve into any personal details. Rather her focus solely lies on the agility of their movement and the way they appreciate the passenger.

The repetition of the term "Lightly" in the very first line describes how softly they bear the palanquin. For the passenger sitting inside, the journey does not seem tiring at any point. The bearers are so swift and light in their movement that it seems they are floating, not treading on the ground.

She sways like.................................the lips of a dream.
In the following lines, Naidu uses a number of metaphors, presented with similes. Firstly, the lady is compared to a flower. By using this comparison, the poet describes how soft the lady is. For the poet, it seems as if the lady is nodding her head as a flower does in the mild air current. Furthermore, the flow of the bearers' song is compared to the wind. So, the lady is swaying with the rhythm of their song.

In the next line, the lady is compared to a bird. The movement of the palanquin seems like the waves and the lady, like a bird, touches the foam while gliding over them. The beautiful metaphor of a stream not only describes the wave-like movement of the palanquin but also depicts how swiftly the bearers carry it.

The third line contains another thought-provoking comparison between the lady and a laugh. According to the speaker, she floats like a laugh from the lips of a dream. In "lips of a dream", the poet uses synecdoche to invest an abstract with a concrete attribute. Here, "dream" represents a dreamer. The lady is like a happy dream of a person. Her transience is compared to the temporary happiness of a dreamer while having a vision of the lady.

Gaily, O gaily...a pearl on a string.

The fifth line begins with a repetition of the term "gaily". It refers to the cheerful mood of the bearers. They are more than happy to carry the lady to her destination. Naidu describes their movement as if they are gliding with the wind. So, here the poet metaphorically compares the bearers to birds or a ship.

While carrying the passenger, they sing to unburden them from weariness. Besides, they bear her like a "pearl on a string". This phrase has two metaphors. First of all, the lady is so precious to the speakers that they think it is like a pearl. This pearl hangs on a string, a metaphorical reference to the poles of the palanquin or the bearers. Imaginatively, the bearers are like a string and the lady, the central attraction, is the pearl hanging on it. So, the bearers along with the passengers depict an image of a pendant.

Softly, O softly...along like a pearl on a string.

The second stanza of "Palanquin Bearers" begins with a refrain. In the beginning, Naidu uses the phrase "Softly, O softly". This line describes how soft the bearers' movement is.

In the following lines, the poet presents a series of comparisons as present in the first stanza. Firstly, the speakers compare the lady to a star. Their song is described as a "dew". Here, the reflection of a star in dew is portrayed. As the dew trembles, it makes the reflection tremble. While the palanquin moves, the passenger's body also shakes in this manner.

Then she is compared to a "beam", meaning a ship or a ray of light. Like a ship sails on the tide, the palanquin is carried. The lady is portrayed as a ship or a light beam that springs on the "brow of the tide". Here, Naidu uses a personal metaphor in the quoted phrase.

In the next line, Naidu hints at the lady's mental state. She is newly married and leaving her home. That's why the poet uses an image of a bride in tears. Apart from that, the last two lines are repeated for the sake of emphasis.

Summary

There is a custom of carrying a bride in a palanquin by the palanquin bearers and the poem 'The Palanquin Bearers' is so finely woven around this custom, which expresses the joy and pride of the palanquin bearers in carrying the newlywed princess to her in-law's house and while walking they are singing along happily.

According to the palanquin bearers, the bride is so light that it feels like the princess is swaying, like a flower sways in the wind. She is sitting in the palanquin and is hearing their song.

They consider the royal princess as a privilege instead of a burden to them since she is sitting and thinking about her future after marriage. Like a flower in the wind, the bride is moving from side to side.

They say that *'she is like the bird that skims on thefoam of a stream'*which means that a bird passes a stream skipping through the foam of the stream and the bride resembles of that bird because she is so delicate to carry.

She carries a mixed feeling as she is leaving her parents behind and moving onto a new phase of her life. She is happy and contented to live and start a new inning with her beloved.

They are carrying her like a pearl on a string since she is precious and delicate like a jewel. In the dew of their song, the princess is hanging like a star. Like a ray of light is seen on the top of a tide, she appears to be jumping just like that.

A tear roll down the eyes of a bride, in the same way, she falls. The bearers are carrying the princess as if she is dew or a teardrop. They are delighted to carry the bride and could not feel her weight because she is very tender.

Question 1. What are the feelings of the palanquin bearers as they carry the princess inside the palanquin?

Answer: The palanquin bearers are delighted as they are carrying a royal bride to her in-laws. As they walk, they feel that she is as delicate like a flower who sways at their song. The palanquin bearers are so careful when they carry her as if she were a pearl on a string. This showcases that they have gained some respect towards her and actually treat her and her emotion delicately.

Question 2. "Lightly, O lightly we bear her along; she sways like a flower in the wind of our song." What are these opening lines suggestive of? Do you think the palanquin bearers are sensitive to the presence of the bride?

Answer: These lines suggest that the bride inside the palanquin is very delicate and light. She is invaluable and also it is the most sacred and auspicious occasion for her.

The palanquin bearers are very sensitive to the presence of the bride as they handle her like a very precious jewel. They are so careful when they carry her as if she were a pearl on a string.

Question 3. What is the poem "Palanquin Bearers" about?

Answer: It is a folk song of the palanquin bearers, typically sung while carrying a newlywed bride. While carrying her to her father's home to the groom's home, bearers often sang such songs in order to cheer the bride up. This song features a variety of epithets used to adorn the delicate beauty of the lady.

Question 4. Why is the bride referred to as "a pearl on a string"?

Answer: By using this phrase, Naidu describes how precious the bride is for the bearers. She is like a pearl, hanging delicately from a string. Here, the string is metaphorically compared to either the palanquin or the bearers. Collectively, they form a pendant and the pearl enhances the value of the chain.

Question 5. What is the meaning of "Palanquin Bearers"?

Answer: The term "Palanquin" originated primarily from East India. It means a covered box, often used for a single passenger. The large box is carried on two horizontal poles by four or six bearers. In this poem, Naidu features the song of such bearers while carrying a lady in the palanquin.

Question 6. In which year the "Palanquin Bearers" was published?

Answer: The poem was first published in London, the United Kingdom in 1896 and later it was published in 1905 in Hyderabad. It appears in Sarojini Naidu's first poetry collection The Golden Threshold.

Question 7. Who sang the poem the "Palanquin Bearers"?

Answer: In this poem, the palanquin bearers sang the song while carrying the bride.

Question 8. What is the tone of the poem "Palanquin Bearers"?

Answer: The tone of this piece remains cheerful, cajoling, and heartwarming throughout. It changes slightly to a sad one in the fourth line of the second verse. However, the poet stylistically maintains the overall tone.

Question 9. What is the mood of "Palanquin Bearers"?

Answer: The mood of this poem is high-spirited, light, and celebratory. This song is sung to cheer the lady up while traveling to her destination.

Question 10.Why do the palanquin bearers carry the bride lightly?

Answer: The bearers, by no means, want to make the bride feel tiresome throughout the journey. Hence, they sing a song while carrying the palanquin as lightly as they can.

Question 11. Why do the palanquin bearers sing?

Answer: The bearers, by no means, want to make the bride feel tiresome throughout the journey. Hence, they sing a song while carrying the palanquin as lightly as they can.

Question 12. How do palanquin bearers carry the bride?

Answer: They carry the bride lightly and softly. Besides, they sing a beautiful song that adorns her features.

Question 13. Who is being carried in the palanquin?

Answer: A newly married lady is carried in the palanquin.

Question 14. How do the palanquin bearers feel while carrying the bride?

Answer: The bearers feel happy in the whole process. They gaily carry the bride as she is a precious gift given to those humble men to take care of.

Question 15. Why is the bride compared to a "flower" and a "bird"?

Answer: The bride's calm and soft features are compared to that of a flower. Besides, the way the palanquin is carried makes it feel that the lady is gliding in the air like a bird.

Question 16. What are the two adverbs used to describe the way the palanquin bearers were carrying their passenger?

Answer: The two adverbs that are used to describe the movement of the bearers are "Lightly" and "Softly".

Question 17. How do we know that the palanquin bearers think that the bride is delicate and must be treasured?

Answer: From the last line of each verse "We bear her along like a pearl on a string", it becomes clear that the bride is delicate and must be treasured.

Question 18. What is the meaning of the expression "a tear from the eyes of a bride"?

Answer: This expression hints at the mental state of the bride. She sheds tears as she is leaving her father's home.

Question 19. What is the message in "Palanquin Bearers" by Sarojini Naidu?

Answer: Through this poem, Naidu conveys an interesting message to readers. It concerns how precious a bride is for the palanquin bearers. They feel blessed to bear her.

Question 20. What does the phrase "brow of the tide" mean?

Answer: This phrase refers to the upper portion of a tide. "Brow" means the summit or peak. It is also a reference to an eyebrow. Hence, this phrase can be interpreted in two ways.

Question 21. What do the palanquin bearers want to mitigate?

Answer: They want to mitigate the bride's sadness as well as her weariness by singing the song.

Question 22. Do you think the palanquin bearers are sensitive to the presence of the bride?

Answer: They are indeed sensitive to the presence of the bride. She is a pearl for them that they are given to take care of.

Question 23. Where are they carrying the palanquin?

Answer: They are carrying the palanquin to the home of the bride's husband.

Question 24. How does the poet describe the movement of the palanquin?

Answer: The poet describes the movement of the palanquin by comparing it to a beam gliding over a stream.

Question 25. What purpose do similes serve in the poem "Palanquin Bearers"?

Answer: In this poem, similes are used to describe the delicacy, softness, and embalming beauty of the lady.

Question 26. Why does the poet refer to bridal laughter and bridal tears?

Answer: The poet refers to the bridal laughter as well as her tears in order to depict the state of a bride's mind. She is happy to begin a new journey. Besides, she feels sad to leave her home for the first time.

Question 27. Why do the palanquin bearers say they carry the palanquin lightly?

Answer: They carry the palanquin lightly as the passenger sitting inside is like an invaluable pearl for them.

Question 28. Why do the palanquin bearers feel privileged?

Answer: They feel privileged to carry the bride. Along the journey, there is none from her family to take care of. Only the bearers are there to protect, cheer and take care of her.

Question 29. What does the poet mean by "lips of a dream"?

Answer: The lady is as transient as a dreamer's laughter. Before marriage, she brought a smile to her parent's faces. After marriage, her presence will bring a smile to her husband's face. In this way, she floats like a peal of laughter from one's face to another's.

Question 30. For what purpose were palanquins used in the past?

Answer: Palanquins were used for transportation in the past. Newly married brides, kings, and queens traveled to faraway places by palanquins.

CHAPTER SEVEN

Woman

by Hira Bansode

She, the river,
Said to him, the sea:
All my life
I have been dissolving myself
and flowing towards you
for your sake
In the end it was I
Who turned into the sea
A woman's gift
Is as large as the sky
But you went on
Worshipping yourself
you never thought
Of becoming a river
And merging
With me.

About the poet

Hira Bansode. born in 1939 in Maharashtra, is one of the early Dalit women writers. She talked for the working class Dalit women who experienced double marginalisation in their work space as well as domestic space. Her poetry carries themes of alienation, freedom from all kinds of bondage and subjugation, estrangement, search of identity and dignity both as a Dalit and as a woman. She often blended ancient myths of women who underwent discrimination with contemporary situations of the Dalit women.

Summary

The poet says that woman is still a slave/ servant (the apt translation of the Marathi word *ghulam* which is the original title of the poem is servant) in spite of the auspicious ritualistic practices which are based on the stories of Sita and Ahalya who were known for their tests and challenges of their chastity. The poet is angry when she states that to be born as a woman in 'unjust' since she is still a slave to everyone regardless of time period. The identity of a woman fades like flowers and her emotions are taken for granted and called as mere 'dreams'. Her desire is not given due importance and her protests are nipped in the bud. A woman is dried up by tradition where her growth is stunted and forever she has to remain as someone's shadow. When festivals celebrate the stories of lords the stories of women in it are painful.

CHAPTER EIGHT

EVIL

By Dinesh Dadhichi

To the best of our knowledge and belief
It is present,
Pervading the pores of society.
We hereby proclaim that we plan to annihilate it,
Every part and every bit.
We shout against it from podia, from rooftops.
It struts and strides and never stops.
To slaughter it, we set out with pomp and glitter;
It simply smiles, has no jolt or jitter.
Often we have seen it, ensconced in the chair,
Sitting cosily across the table,
But before we can touch it,
It's already flowing in our bloodstream.
It's snugly perched on the hand
That brandishes the sword against it.
The arrows almed at it
Find their way into the very core of our being.
Tired and vanquished,
We solemnly reiterate
To the best of our knowledge and belief,
It is present, pervading the pores of the universe
And our fight against it goes on.

SUMMARY

In this poem poet says that we often doings to put on end but it is present every where. People should for the destruction of the evil from the rooftops. But still remains to everywhere in the society. No part of society is free from this evil. It is present in this evil. It is present in everywhere human being and effects their nature so body that it remains in their heart without their knowledge.

To destory the evil people. Setup realise with enthusiasm. But it doesn't put effect an evil. It simply smiles and has no fear or regret evil in present in the office also. It takes places in the mind of the officers. Who are sitting comfortably on the chair. But when anybody tries to point or through all it is felt that the person is affected by the evil.

Dinesh Dadhichi occupies a very great place in the history of English literature. In this poem, the poet describes here a social evil. It takes place in the mind of the officers who are sitting comfortably on the chair. Whenever tries to attack the evil it enters into the body of the person and make him evil. In the last stanza the poet says that after doing all effort to do the story the evil one feel tried and affected.

CHAPTER NINE

Active Voice and Passive Voice

Active and Passive Voice Rules, Example, Exercise

Active Voice	Passive Voice (Auxiliary Verb – is/am/are)
Subject + V1+s/es+ object	Object+ is/am/are+ V3+ by + subject
Subject + Do/does+ not – V1 + Object	Object + is/am/are+ not + V3+ by Subject
Does+ Subject+ V1+Object+?	Is/am/are + Object+ V3+ by subject +?

Active and Passive Voice Rules for Present Simple Tense

Active and Passive Voice Example with Answers of Present Simple Tense

Active: He reads a novel.
Passive: A novel is read.
Active: He does not cook food.
Passive: Food is not cooked by him.
Active: Does he purchase books?
Passive: Are books purchased by him?

Active: They grow plants.
Passive: Plants are grown by them.
Active: She teaches me.
Passive: I am taught by her.

<table>
<tr><td align="center">Active Voice</td><td align="center">Passive Voice
(Auxiliary Verb- is/am/are + being)</td></tr>
<tr><td align="center">Subject + is/am/are+ v1+ ing + object</td><td align="center">Object+ is/am/are+ being+ V3+ by + subject</td></tr>
<tr><td align="center">Subject + is/am/are+ not+ v1+ ing+ object</td><td align="center">Object + is/am/are+ not + being+V3+ by Subject</td></tr>
<tr><td align="center">Is/am/are+ subject+v1+ing + object+?</td><td align="center">Is/am/are + Object+ V3+ by subject +?</td></tr>
</table>

Active and Passive Voice Rules for Present Continuous Tense

Active and Passive Voice Exercises of Present Continuous Tense

Active: Esha is singing a song.
Passive: A song is being sung by Esha.
Active: Kritika is not chopping vegetables.
Passive: Vegetables are not being chopped by Kritika.
Active: Is Ritika buying a table?
Passive: Is a table being bought by Ritika?
Active: They are serving poor people.
Passive: Poor people are being served by them.
Active: She is disturbing Dinesh.
Passive: Dinesh is being disturbed by her.

Active Voice	Passive Voice (Auxiliary Verb- has/have +been)
Subject + has/have+ v3+ object	Object- has/have+ been- V3+ by + subject
Subject + has/have- not- v3+ object	Object + has/have- not + been-V3+ by Subject
Has/have+ subject+ v3 + object-?	Has/Have + Object+ been+V3- by subject +?

Active and Passive Voice Rules for Present Perfect Tense

Active and Passive Voice Example with Answers of Present Perfect Tense

Active: Nitesh has challenged her.
Passive: She has been challenged by Nitesh.
Active: Radhika has not written an article.
Passive: An article has not been written by Radhika.
Active: Have they left the apartment?
Passive: Has apartment been left by them?
Active: She has created this masterpiece.
Passive: This masterpiece has been created by her.
Active: I have read the newspaper.
Passive: The newspaper has been read by me.

Active Voice	Passive Voice (Auxiliary Verb- was/were)
Subject + V2+ object	Object+ was/were V3+ by + subject
Subject +did+ not+v1+ object	Object + was/were+ not +V3+ by Subject
Did+ subject+V1+ object+?	Was/were + Object+ V3+ by subject +?

Active and Passive Voice Rules for Past Simple Tense

Active and Passive Voice Exercises of Past Simple Tense

Active: Reema cleaned the floor.
Passive: The floor was cleaned by Reema.
Active: Aisha bought a bicycle.
Passive: A bicycle was bought by Aisha.
Active: Naman called my friends.
Passive: My friends were called by Naman.
Active: I saved him.
Passive: He was saved by me.
Active: Miraya paid the bills.
Passive: The bills were paid by Miraya.

Active Voice	Passive Voice (Auxiliary Verb- was/were + being)
Subject + was/were + v1+ing+ object.	Object+ was/were +being+V3+ by + subject
Subject +was/were+ not+v1+ing + object	Object + was/were+ not +being+V3+ by Subject
Was/were+ Subject + V1+ing + object+?	Was/were + Object+ being+v3+ by+ subject+?

Active and Passive Voice Rules for Past Continuous Tense

Active and Passive Voice Examples with Answers of Past Continuous Tense

Active: Nitika was painting the wall.
Passive: The wall was being painted by Nitika.
Active: Manish was repairing the car.
Passive: The car was being repaired by Manish.
Active: Were you reciting the poem?
Passive: Was the poem being recited?
Active: She was baking the cake.
Passive: The cake was being baked by her.
Active: She was watching me.
Passive: I was being watched by her.

Active Voice	Passive Voice (Auxiliary Verb- had +been)
Subject + had + v3+ object.	Object+ had+been +V3+ by – subject
Subject +had+ not+v3– object	Object – had+ not +been+V3– by Subject
Had+ Subject + V3+ object+?	Had – Object+ been+v3– by+ subject+?

Active and Passive Voice Rules for Past Perfect Tense

Active and Passive Voice Exercises of Past Perfect Tense

Active: Misha had cleaned the floor.
Passive: The floor had been cleaned by Misha.
Active: Vidhi had not received the parcel.
Passive: The parcel had not been received by Vidhi.
Active: Vishal had solved the doubt.

Passive: The doubt had been solved.
Active: Had they caught the thief?
Passive: Had the thief been caught by them?
Active: I had paid fifty thousand.
Passive: Fifty thousand had been paid by me.

Active Voice	Passive Voice (Auxiliary Verb- will+ be)
Subject + will+ v1+ object.	Object+ will+ be +V3+ by + subject
Subject +will + not+ V1+object	Object + will+ not +be+V3+ by Subject
Will+ Subject + V1+ object+?	Will + Object+ be +v3+ by+ subject+?

Active and Passive Voice Rules for Future Simple Tense

Active and Passive Voice Examples with Answers of Future Simple Tense

Active: Kriya will sew the bag.
Passive: The bag will be sewed by Kriya.
Active: Disha will not arrange the things.
Passive: The things will not be arranged by Disha.
Active: Will you mop the floor?
Passive: Will the floor be mopped by you?
Active: They will post the letter.
Passive: The letter will be posted.
Active: Reena will save money.
Passive: Money will be saved by Reena.

Active Voice	Passive Voice
Subject – will+ have +v3+ object.	Object+ will+ have+ been +V3+ by + subject
Subject – will+ have +not+v3+ object.	Object – will+ have –not–been–v3– subject
Will– Subject+have+v3– object–?	Will + object–have–been+v3+by –subject+?

Active and Passive Voice Rules for Future Perfect Tense

Active and Passive Voice Exercises of Future Perfect Tense

Active: They will have brought the toy.
Passive: The toy will have been brought by them.
Active: Nimesh will not have changed the table cover.
Passive: The table cover will not have been changed by Nimesh.
Active: Will she have written the notes.
Passive: Will the notes have been written by her?
Active: They will have won the match.
Passive: The match will have been won by them.
Active: Vijay will have washed a shirt.
Passive: A shirt will have been washed by Vijay.

CHAPTER TEN

Prepositions

Rules Of Prepositions

A preposition is a word or a set of words that indicates the location or some other relation between a noun or a pronoun and other parts of the sentence. The rules of prepositions and their correct usage go as follows:

Preposition Rules – 1 – Preposition must have an object – a preposition is not a preposition unless it goes with a related noun or a pronoun that is the object of the preposition. A preposition is always with an object – without an object, it is an adverb that never has an object. Lets us understand with examples –

- He is **in the kitchen.** (preposition 'in' has object the kitchen)
- You may come **in.** (adverb 'in' has no object; it qualifies come)
- Thcre was a car **before me.** (preposition 'before' has object 'me')
- Ram has never seen it **before.** (adverb 'before' has no object; it qualifies seen)
- We will catch up **after the gym.** (preposition 'after' has object 'gym')
- They called soon **after.** (adverb 'after' has no object; it qualifies 'called')

Preposition Rules – 2- Must be placed before – As the name says 'Pre-Position' – it comes before something. Generally, but not always, a preposition goes before a noun or a pronoun. Understand with examples –

- I put the things **in the box.** ('in' is placed before the noun ''box')

You do not end a sentence with a preposition is one of the undying myths of English Grammar because even when a preposition is not placed before its object, it is closely related to its object. For example –

- **Whom** did you talk **to?** (Preposition 'to' related to the pronoun 'Whom')

Preposition Rules – 3 – The Pronoun following the Preposition should be an object form. The noun or pronoun following a preposition forms a prepositional object. If a pronoun is following a preposition, it should be in the objective form (me, her, them) and not the subjective form like (I, she, they, etc.). See the examples below-

- The gift was **from them.** (preposition 'from' followed by the objective pronoun 'them')
- The secret is **between him** and **her.** (preposition 'between' followed by the objective pronoun 'him')

Preposition Rules – 4 (A)- Avoid 'like' when a verb is involved. The preposition 'like' that means "similar to" should be followed by a noun, pronoun, noun phrase as an object of the preposition. A subject or a verb should not follow the preposition 'like'. For example –

- Correct – She looks **like** her **mother.** (noun 'mother' is the object of the preposition 'like')

- Incorrect – She looks **like** her **mother does.** (avoid 'like' with noun + verb)

*4 (B) – When there is a comparison between a subject or verb, **instead of like,** use as, as if, as though, or 'the way'. Taking the same sentence as an example –*

- Incorrect – She looks like her mother does.
- Correct – She looks the way her mother does.

   More examples–

- Incorrect – Do like he asks.
- Correct – Do as he asks.
- Incorrect – She looks like she is angry.
- Correct – She looks as if she is angry.

4(C) – Unless there is a verb involved, do not use 'as'. 'As' means "in the same manner" so avoid using preposition 'as' if the verb is not involved. Check the examples –

- Incorrect: I, as most people, try to use good words in English.
- Correct: I, as most people do, try to use good words in English. Or I, like most people, try to use good words in English.

Preposition Rules – 5 – Do not confuse preposition 'to' with infinitive 'to'. *'To' is an infinitive participle (to sing, to dance, etc.) as well as a preposition too like (to me, to Moscow, etc.). Understand the difference between the two with the help of examples –*

'To' as a preposition-

- I am used **to** swimming.
- I look forward **to** seeing you. (not 'see you')

'To' as an infinitive participle –

- I used **to live** in Australia.
- They love **to dance.**

Preposition Rules – 6 – *Some words that look like verbs follow the preposition 'to'.* **A Verb cannot be an object of a preposition.** *This rule of preposition may seem confusing, so let us understand with examples –*

- I like **to swim.**
- These goggles are **for swimming.**

In these examples, "swim" and "swimming" are not acting as verbs.

In the first example, to swim is part of the infinitive that occurs when a verb is used as a noun, adverb or an adjective. Here, to swim is a thing that the person likes doing, not an action that is being performed.

In the second example, swimming is a gerund which is a noun though it is formed out of a verb. Here, swimming is a thing to which goggles are related. No one in this sentence is performing the act of swimming.

Preposition Rules – 7 – Do not confuse preposition 'In' and 'Into'. *This rule of preposition says, use "into" to express motion toward something and reserve the preposition "in" when you want to indicate a location. See the example for clarity –*

- I swam **in** the pool. (Indicating location)
- Look **in** the almirah. (Indicating location)
- The cat jumped **into** the well. (Expressing motion)
- He drove **into** the city. (Expressing motion)

CHAPTER ELEVEN

Idioms

Idioms - Related to Colours

1. Out of the blue– randomly, without warning, surprisingly
Example: "That storm came out of the blue and I didn't have an umbrella!"

2. Green with envy– to be very jealous, envious
Example: "Katie was green with envy when she saw you got a new car for your birthday."

3. Gray area– something that is unclear, undefined
Example: The issue of allowing mobile phones in the classroom is a gray area right now- it could go either way.

4. Caught red-handed– to catch someone in the act of doing something
Example: "He was caught red-handed while stealing those candy bars."

5. Green thumb– to be skilled at gardening
Example: "My mother has a green thumb- she can make anything grow!"

6. Black sheep– to be the outcast, odd one out, unlike the others
Example: "Rachel is the black sheep in the family because she is an artist whereas everyone else is an economist."

7. Once in a blue moon– very rarely
Example: "Once in a blue moon you will see that mean professor smile."

8. Take the red eye– a late night flight that arrives early in the morning
Example: "I took the red eye from California to New York last night and now I am exhausted."

9. Tickled pink– to be extremely pleased
Example: "Your grandma was tickled pink that you called on her birthday!"

10. White lie– a small lie that is told to be polite or avoid hurting someone's feelings

Example: "I didn't like her dress, but I told a white lie because I didn't want to offend her.

11. To catch someone red-handed - to see someone doing something they shouldn't be doing

Example: "Bobby promised he wouldn't eat any more biscuits, but when I went into the kitchen, I caught him red-handed opening a new packet."

12. See red - to become very angry very suddenly

Example: "When Jenny told me she'd broken Mum's glasses, I saw red and screamed at her."

13. To be in the red - to be in debt/owe people money; the opposite to "in the black"

Example: "Uncle Tam is always in the red because he borrows money from relatives for his bad business ideas."

14. Raise a red flag - a warning

Example: "Her reaction when she lost the chess match raised a red flag as to how she deals with conflict."

15. Paint the town red - have a night out with lots of fun

Example: "When the pop star finished his concert, he headed out to paint the town red."

16. Roll out the red carpet - give someone a very warm welcome, with very special treatment

Example: "When the Chief Executive came to our school, we really rolled out the red carpet, and showed him how great our students are."

17. In the black - to have some money; the opposite to "in the red

Example: "Ever since I started my part-time job, my bank account is always in the black."

18. The pot calling the kettle black - when you accuse another person of doing things that the you are guilty of doing

Example: "John telling Tom to smile more is a case of the pot calling the kettle black – I don't think I've ever seen John smile!"

19. Black out - to faint

Example: "Donald blacked out after scoring that goal. We were really worried he might have been injured, but it turns out he just hadn't eaten all day."

20. Black and white - very clear what is right and what is wrong

Example: "War is not a black and white issue."

21. Put something down in black and white - record something in a written or printed form, to make it more official
Example: "I'm not quitting my job until I get the offer for the new position down in black and white".

22. Bolt from the blue - when news comes unexpectedly
Example: "My grandparents' divorce was a bolt from the blue. I always thought they were so happy."

23. The blues - feeling unhappy
Example: "Whenever my holidays end I get the blues."

24. blue in the face - used especially about arguments; for a very long time, usually with no solution
Example: "Mum and Aunty Joan argued until they were blue in the face about what to do for Grandpa's birthday, and didn't plan anything. In the end, he threw his own party!"

25. The grass is always greener on the other side - other people's lives always seem better than your own – but they're probably not
Example: "June was so jealous of Eric's new job at Google despite being quite senior at Facebook. The grass is always greener on the other side, after all."

26. Green-eyed monster - jealousy
Example: "Barry's been feeling like the green-eyed monster since his ex-girlfriend started dating a pop star."

27. Give the green light - let someone do something
Example: "Mum and Dad have given us the green light to go to the music festival in Tokyo!"

28. To have a heart of gold - to be very kind and generous
Example: "The charity committee have hearts of gold: they're all volunteering at an orphanage in Suzhou for the whole summer holiday."

29. Grey area - a situation that is not clear, or where the rules are not known
Example: "The new school rules on hair are a bit of a grey area. It's not clear if you're allowed to dye it if it's a natural colour."

30. Born with a silver spoon in your mouth - born into a rich family
Example: "Charlotte was born with a silver spoon in her mouth. Her grandparents bought her a Ferrari for her 18th birthday!"

31. A white lie - a lie that is told to stop someone being upset or affected by the truth
Example: "I told Grandma a little white lie about what I'm doing at the

weekend – I don't want her guessing about the surprise dinner!"

32. Black Market - buying and selling something illegally, particularly something that is difficult or impossible to obtain otherwise

Example: "His latest movie is not in cinemas yet but I was able to get a copy on the black market."

33. Blackleg - somebody who breaks the rules of a strike, somebody who is going against his fellow workers during a strike

Example: "For three months, while the big strike of the engineers was in progress, Green, who was a blackleg, decided to work."

34. To Get The Green Light - to grant or to receive permission to do something

Example: "I submitted that project last week and the boss told me today that I got the green light to start. I'm really excited."

35. To Be Green With Envy - to have a desire to have something that somebody else has and wish you would have that

Example: "I was green with envy when I saw John new set of golf clubs."

36. Grey Matter - we use this expression to refer to our intellect or our brains

Example: "Why don't you sit down or spend a few hours or even a night thinking about it using your grey matter."

37. Black And White - something that is pretty obvious, something that you can see and understand quite clearly like old-fashioned newspapers

Example: "I think it's black and white, really. It's quite easy to understand. It shouldn't present any problems for anybody."

38. In The Red - it's a reference to our bank accounts. So usually when we're in the red means we have overdrawn a bank account. We have no money.

Example: "I'm in the red again. It always happens to me in the last few days of the month."

39. To pass with flying colours - to do extremely well

Example: "I'm so proud of Tania. She was so worried about her HKDSE, but she passed with flying colours, and won a scholarship to university!"

40. Yellow-bellied - describes someone who is a coward

Example: "I wanted Jamie to come on Space Mountain with me, but he's such a yellow-bellied baby."

Idioms of Culture

1. Apple of one's Eye : Object of Love

2. At the Eleventh Hour : At the last stage

3. A man of spirits: Courageous Man

4. To provide one's mettle: Courage and determination to do something Difficult

5. To beat about the Bush : to say something in a roundabout manner

6. To burn the midnight oil : to work hard

7. To break the Ice : To break the silence

8. A bed of roses : Full of happiness

9. A big Gun : An important person

10. To bury the hatchet : To end the Enimity

11. To burn the candle at both ends : To overspend Money and energy

12. Damoclesn Sword : An impending Danger

13. A cock and bull Story : Imaginary story

14. A fair weather friend: A selfish friend

15. To get on one's Nerve : To be source of worry

16. Gala Day : Day of Rejoicing

17. Hale and hearty : Healthy and sound

18. Dark Horse : A man of unknown capability

19. To gird up one's loins : To prepare oneself for work

20. To come with flying colours: To succeed with credit

21. Hallmark : Genuine Excellence

22. A herculean task : difficult task

23. To makes amends for : To compensate

24. To eat a humble pie : offer humble apology

25. Hard of hearings : Somewhat deaf

26. To go Bananas : to become angry

27. A nasty taste in mouth: to be angry after a bad experience

28. To have two left feet : awkward in moving or dancing

29. To pour hearts : to tell feelings

30. Have itchy feet : To travel

31. To keep up with the joneses : to trying having new possessions

32. To turn a new leaf : to change yourself to become better

33. To line your pockets: to make youself reacher

34. A bitter pill to swallow : unpleasant but to be accepted

35. Put the records straight: to tell the facts

36. To work like magic : work immediately

37. To know where one stands : to know your position

38. Drive someone up the wall : make someone very angry

39. Send the cat among the pigeons : do or say something that make a lot of people

40. Dug into a hole : to cause a problem that is difficult to escape

CHAPTER TWELVE

Letter Writing – Orders and Complaints

Order Letter Format

Sender's Address

____

____

____

Date

Receiver's Address

____

____

____

Subject: _______________________________________

Dear Sir/Ma'am,

Body of the Letter

Paragraph 1 – Introduction and Purpose of Writing the Letter.

Paragraph 2 – List of items required with the quantity in bullet points or tabular columns.

Paragraph 3 – Concluding paragraph stating when you expect the delivery of items and thanking them for their service.

Complimentary closing – Yours sincerely, Sincerely, etc.

Signature of the sender

NAME in block letters

Letter: Placing Order for Books for School Library

You are Anoop/Akriti, Baden Power Senior Secondary School, Delhi. Write a letter to the Sales Manager, Aparna Publishing House, placing an order for the books (minimum four titles) for your school library. Invent the necessary details.

GPS Public School
Delhi
    25 July, 20××
    The Sales Manager
Aparna Publishing House
Delhi
    Subject: Order for Books
    Sir/Madam
    I would like to place an order for the following books for our school library.

S.No.	Name of Books	Authors	Copies required
1	Great Expecations	Charles Dickens	20
2	Crime and Punishment	Fyodor Dostoyevsky	30
3	The Invisible Man	H G Wells	25
4	Pride and Prejudice	Jane Austen	40
5	Alice in Wonderland	Lewis Carol	15
6	Animal Farm	George Orwell	25

Kindly supply the books by next week. Also, please make sure that the books are in good condition and arrive undamaged.

I request you to send the bill along with the books after applying the discount permissible to schools. Payment will be made soon after the receipt and checking of the books.

Damaged books will not be accepted nor any payment will be made for the same.

We seek your cooperation in this regard.
Thank you
Yours faithfully
Akriti Sharma
Librarian

Letter of Placing Order for Ordering: Sports Accessories

Mr. Ravi Saxena is the Sports Instructor of DAV Public School, Kalka. The Principal has asked him to place an order for buying volleyball nets, cricket bats, tennis racquets and tennis balls, footballs and necessary sports accessories. Mr Ravi Saxena places an order with M/s Youth Sports Equipment, Rohini, New Delhi. Write the order letter.

Kalka

March 5, 2020
The Manager
M/s Youth Sports Equipment
Sector-7, Rohini
New Delhi
Subject: Order for sports items and accessories
Sir

I am the Sports Instructor of my school and I would like to place an order for the following sports items and accessories.

1. Volleyball nets 6 pieces
2. Cricket bats 4 pieces
3. Tennis racquets4 pieces
4. Tennis balls 2 pieces
5. Footballs6 pieces
6. Leg-guards12 pieces
7. Gloves 6 pairs

We expect a reasonable discount which you allow for educational institutions. Make sure the items are of high quality. Please despatch the above items at our earliest. The payment would be sent through bank draft within a week after the supply is received.

Yours sincerely,

Ravi Saxena

(Sports Instructor)

Complaint Letter Sample 1 – Poor Maintenance of the Garden and Improper Waste Disposal

45 B, Rory Lane

Damsel Street

Mumbai – 400056

29th December, 2021

The Secretary

Residential Association

Mumbai – 400056

Subject: Complaint letter regarding the poor maintenance of the garden and improper waste disposal

Sir,

I am Shawn Mendez, a resident of Rory Lane. I am writing to bring to your notice the poor maintenance of the garden around our residential area and the improper disposal of waste. The garden around the residential area was watered regularly, and grass shrubs were trimmed and maintained neatly in the beginning. It has been more than a month now since any kind of maintenance is done in the garden. We have tried contacting the person in charge, but every effort has just been in vain.

Another growing issue is the problem of waste disposal. There were people from the corporation collecting garbage for disposal every two days, but it has been more than a week now since they have collected any garbage from our area. This has led to the accumulation of waste, and people have started dumping it in the corner of the street as they have no other choice. Kindly look into this and the maintenance of the garden as it would become a huge mess if this continues. It would be highly appreciated if you could also inform the residents that all garbage would be collected and not to throw them out around the street corners.

Thank you in advance.

Yours faithfully,

Signature

SHAWN MENDEZ

Complaint Letter Sample 2 – Damaged Product Received

5/652, SNV Street
VKL Colony
Hyderabad – 500025
November 26, 2021
The Manager
Customer Service Department
Taurus Shop
New Delhi – 110023
Subject: Complaint about a damaged product received
Sir/Ma'am,

I had purchased a black top from your online store. I received the product today, and I tried filing a return request as the size is smaller than the one I had ordered, and the cloth is torn on the left side. For some reason, the return request is not being filed. The page is either getting redirected or stuck. I have tried multiple times, and I could not go through with it. Can you please check and let me know if the return request has been filed for the order no. 3049. If not, kindly let me know what I should do to return the product.

I am attaching herewith photographs of the damaged portion of the top and the opening video for your reference.

Thank you
Yours sincerely,
Signature
SINDHU SHANKAR

Complaint Letter Sample 3 – Installation of New Street Lights

12B, Nelson Manickam Road
Nungambakkam
Chennai – 600045
13/12/2021
The Councillor
Ward No. 26

Chennai – 600052

Subject: Regarding installation of new street lights in our area

Sir,

I am writing to bring to your kind attention that there are no street lights in our area and it has become a huge problem as it has started raining. It is very difficult for people who travel through this area because it is very dark at night, and with continuous rains, the place floods up. It becomes really difficult to drive as the roads are damaged, and there have been constant accidents because of this. Therefore, I request you to kindly take some action at the earliest and install street lights in our area as it is a danger if left like this.

Thank you for your time and cooperation in advance.

Yours faithfully,

Signature

DERRICK RAJ

CHAPTER THIRTEEN

Writing Agendas of a Meeting

Meeting Agenda :

When conducting a business meeting, you might need to manage a large number of tasks and individuals. A successful meeting agenda may assist you in discussing all the required content and keeping the meeting on schedule. In this article, we explain how to write a meeting agenda that is effective for your team, discuss the important items to include in the agenda and provide a sample of a meeting agenda to help you lead a meeting.

or

A meeting agenda is a list of topics or activities that you want to cover during the meeting. The primary aim of the agenda is to provide attendees with a clear picture of what will happen during the meeting, who will lead each task and how long each step may take. Having this knowledge before and during the meeting can support an effective discussion.

write a meeting agenda :

Whether you have a short one-hour meeting or one that lasts several hours, you can use these steps to help you write an agenda:

1. Identify the meeting's goal : When you start with your goal, you can ensure that the meeting's purpose is clear and that every activity you wish to do meets your objective. Creating a meeting goal can help the participants stay as attentive as possible. A meeting goal to approve the company's monthly advertising budget, for example, is more realistic than a goal to reduce total spending.

2. Seek input from the participants : If you want to keep your attendees involved throughout the meeting, get their feedback ahead of time so you can make sure the meeting meets their needs. You may ask them to share their questions regarding the topics or can address any suggestions they have. Once you get a list of suggestions from the participants, you can review them and select which ones to use.

3. Prepare the list of questions that you want to address : To create a list of questions for the meeting, you may start by understanding your meeting's goal. Then you may review the subjects you want to address. On some agendas, a topic is merely a phrase, such as "rental equipment." However, by expressing discussion points as questions, you may explain the objective of each agenda item. These prompts can help you assure you are inviting conversation and obtaining all the data you need for each agenda item.

4. Determine the goal of each task : It is best practice to make sure each task you do during your meeting has a specific goal. These goals may be to provide information, get feedback or make a choice. Note the reason for each task as you move through your schedule. This phase will assist meeting participants in understanding when you need their opinion and when you need to make a decision.

5. Calculate how much time you will spend on each task : This section of the agenda guarantees that you have adequate time to cover all the items on your agenda. It also aids the participants in fitting their remarks and questions within the allotted time.

You can optimise your timeframe by giving more time to items you anticipate taking longer to discuss or scheduling items of higher importance earlier in the discussion to ensure vital topics are covered. If you have many team members coming to your meeting, you may even limit time on certain topics to streamline the conversation, encourage a quick decision and keep the meeting on schedule.

6. Attach documents : Attaching documents related to the topics in the agenda can help the participants understand the subject. You can also save time for participants who would otherwise have to search on their computers for these documents. It also makes it easier for you when you're conducting the meeting.

7. Identify who leads each topic : Usually, the leaders take the leading role in a meeting, whereas in some cases, the team members lead the meeting under the supervision of the leaders. You may assign topics to relevant individuals beforehand. This step helps keep the meeting productive and ensures that everyone is prepared for their responsibilities.

8. End each meeting with a review : Leaving time to end each meeting with a review can help participants better understand what decisions they made and what information they discussed so they can take any necessary steps after the meeting. During this review, you and other meeting participants might also consider answering what went well during the meeting and what needs improvement.

Advantages of writing a meeting agenda

Some of the major advantages of writing a meeting agenda are:

1. By sharing the agenda ahead of time, participants of the meeting may duly prepare to address the issues.
2. Having a meeting agenda helps in quick decision making.
3. A meeting agenda helps in guaranteeing that all the issues you want to discuss in the meeting are covered.
4. Meeting agendas save time by avoiding unnecessary discussions.
5. A meeting agenda aids in the preparation of meeting minutes and resolutions.
6. By preparing a meeting agenda, the meeting members can discuss their thoughts and views informally before the meeting.

Things to include in a meeting agenda

Some of the most important items you can include in your meeting agenda include:

- **Meeting schedule:** Include the meeting time, date and venue and add the names of anybody who will attend the meeting.
- **Title:** The titles are crucial in any agenda because they help the participants identify the topics.
- **Objective:** The objective of the meeting can also be stated in the agenda to remind attendees what the meeting is about and what it intends to accomplish.

- **Overview:** Include a list of all subjects or activities that need to be discussed during the meeting. Every topic or activity can have a time limit to ensure you can discuss all important topics.
- **Housekeeping:** This section contains a welcome note, introductions and any absent apologies if applicable.
- **Informational items:** This includes any new information you would like to share with the group.
- **Items to do:** This is a list of actions that your group should do during or after the meeting.
- **Topics for discussion:** These are the issues on which you would like your team's input.
- **Call to action:** You may include a call to action that marks the beginning and end of the meeting on the agenda.

Tips for creating a meeting agenda

Follow the below tips to create your meeting agenda for best results:

1. Send out the agenda three to four days before the meeting : Sending the agenda a few days before the meeting may help the participants to prepare for the meeting and also give them some time to complete any task that is required for a successful session. However, sending it too soon can lead it getting lost in the employee's inbox.

2. Proofread the agenda before sending it out : Some meeting participants may rely significantly on the agenda, and it may be a good idea to review it for mistakes and completeness before sending it out. Proofreading ensures that the agenda has all the necessary information and also helps in reflecting your attention to detail. Proper spelling and grammar ensure that attendees understand the message you are delivering.

3. Take advantage of online templates : There are many online templates available with word processing applications. Many word processing applications provide templates for a wide range of personal and professional documents, including meeting agendas. Consider using one of these if you are not sure how to begin.

4. Use bullet points : Rather than providing paragraphs of material in your meeting agenda, consider using bullet points to list any topics for discussion or important updates you want to share. Bullet points are often more scannable than paragraphs and help in clearly mentioning the details of the meeting. You can even use sub-bullets to go into more detail.

Meeting agenda sample

You can use the following sample meeting schedule when crafting your own agenda:

Meeting Agenda
Date: July 4, 2021
Time: 1:00 PM IST
Location: Conference Room
Agenda details
Goals: Examine last year's marketing efforts, identify seasonal slumps in product demand, plan methods to raise demand during these slumps and make sure we are ready for the next marketing campaign.

1. Examine last year's marketing initiatives
Time: 15 minutes
Purpose: Share information
Leader: Raj Mehra

a. Showcase previous year's marketing initiatives

b. After each marketing campaign, review the sales figures

c. Determine which campaigns had the greatest impact

2. How can we effectively handle our product's evolving needs?
Time: 45 minutes
Purpose: Discussion
Leader: Bhanu Saxena

a. Examine sales figures from the previous four quarters

b. Recognise any patterns in the sales figures

c. Discuss ways to increase sales

3. Getting ready for the next marketing campaign
Time: 20 minutes
Purpose: Decision
Leader: Riya Gupta

a. How should we prepare for the upcoming marketing campaign?

i. Review the marketing campaign materials that are attached

ii. Assign duties to each member of the team

b. How will we measure the campaign's effectiveness?

c. Review the campaign's sales targets

4. Finalising of meeting

Time: 5 minutes

Purpose: Decision

Leader: Raj Mehra

    a. What did we do well in this meeting?

    b. How should we approach the next meeting?